BERKLEE PRESS

THE PRIVATE GUITAR STUDIO HANDBOOK

STRATEGIES AND POLICIES FOR A PROFITABLE MUSIC BUSINESS

MIKE MCADAM

Berklee Press

Editor in Chief: Jonathan Feist
Vice President of Online Learning and Continuing Education: Debbie Cavalier
Assistant Vice President of Operations for Berklee Media: Robert F. Green
Assistant Vice President of Marketing and Recruitment for Berklee Media: Mike King
Dean of Continuing Education: Carin Nuernberg
Editorial Assistants: Matthew Dunkle, Reilly Garrett, Zoë Lustri
Cover Design: Ranja Karifilly, Small Mammoth Design

ISBN: 978-0-87639-144-0

1140 Boylston Street
Boston, MA 02215-3693 USA
(617) 747-2146

Visit Berklee Press Online at
www.berkleepress.com

Study with
■ **BERKLEE ONLINE**

online.berklee.edu

DISTRIBUTED BY

HAL•LEONARD®
CORPORATION
7777 W. BLUEMOUND RD. P.O. BOX 13819
MILWAUKEE, WISCONSIN 53213

Visit Hal Leonard Online at
www.halleonard.com

Berklee Press, a publishing activity of Berklee College of Music, is a not-for-profit educational publisher.
Available proceeds from the sales of our products are contributed to the scholarship funds of the college.

CONTENTS

ACKNOWLEDGMENT

I never thought I would be a music teacher. To be fair, I didn't know what I would "be." All I knew is that I wanted to take advantage of every musical opportunity that I could. So, when I had the opportunity to start teaching guitar, I found that it was a great way to work with people while keeping me close to my instrument.

I was unprepared in every way. Despite this, teaching was fun and I wanted to be good at it. I am fortunate to have worked with some great instructors, and I felt like I could strive to reach the same level. I want to thank all of them.

I would also like to thank the hundreds of students I have had the pleasure of working with over the years. Though I was being paid to teach lessons, you often taught me much more. The relationships I have built over the years have been by far, the most fulfilling part of this work. I am thankful for this every day.

I would like to thank all the musicians who contributed to this book. It was a pleasure to discuss our profession, and it did not take me long to see why you are so inspiring to others. It was great working with so many talented people who were so willing to share their gifts.

And lastly, I would like to thank Robyn Neville for helping me with this book and being so supportive in its creation.

—Mike McAdam

INTRODUCTION

There are many books on the market that focus on the how-to's of starting your own private music lessons business. Several are very good, but I wanted this book to deal with some of the issues I didn't see covered in any of them. I had to go far outside the realm of normal teaching books to find something that dealt with the mechanics of business that would apply to private lessons. While this book will offer my own insights into common issues, I wanted to provide the tools a teacher can use to grow his or her own business, and make the business easier to run on a day-to-day basis.

MY STORY

When I started playing the guitar in 1987, I found my sustaining passion. Throughout the 1990s, I played in several bands, one of which was successful enough to release CDs internationally and perform on two European tours. I enrolled in Berklee College of Music in 2000. Going to Berklee was a lifelong dream.

A friend of mine suggested I take a class called "The Private Teacher," a course dedicated to the fundamental ideas of how to build and sustain a lessons business. While I was taking the class, I had another student approach me about lessons. I took the opportunity and used him as a guinea pig, applying what I had learned in the class to his lessons. I was a senior at Berklee, and like many people at that stage in their education, I had *no* idea what the hell I would be doing when I graduated!

I started to see that teaching could be a viable way to support myself in the music business, so in 2003, I began giving lessons professionally. Slowly, I built my student base to three days a week while I performed and kept my serving job for extra money and benefits. I took an additional teaching job at another studio and had about fifty-five students a week.

In 2005, I was putting together a performing guitar group and was looking for commercial space to rehearse in. While I was looking at various locations, I realized that renting commercial space was easier and less expensive than I originally thought. The rent was easily covered by the students I currently taught, so it became possible to take on even more students.

Within the next two years, my business grew again, and I no longer had any lessons times available for new students—a good problem to have! So, I hired another instructor to help build the business. Since 2007, I have added another ten instructors and have opened a second school. In addition to the guitar, we added piano, drums, and voice.

It is amazing how quickly my business moved from teaching a couple of kids lessons in my bedroom to its present state. I truly believe that if you put just a few of the principles I lay out in this book into practice, it will help you to become a better teacher, and help you to run your business more efficiently and profitably. I love teaching, and it is a big part of my life. However, I don't want my business to run me, and that is the true motivation for this book.

As business theorist Jim Rohn said, "Success leaves clues." I have included some case studies of other music teachers that can hopefully shed some light on these concepts. Not all of them are guitarists. I have done this not only because their stories are applicable to any music lessons studio, but as a reminder to always look outside of your zone to find things that can work for you.

Some of the information in this book may seem harsh. This is the reality of when any arts endeavor and business intermingle. Not always the greatest dance partners!

My own experiences along with the hundreds of teachers and students I have worked with over the years, confirm this. I offer these insights as an opportunity to help you make as few mistakes as possible while pursing your dreams.

CHAPTER 1

Starting Your Studio

"Doing any career takes time and effort, but doing music requires you to work harder. It's not a 9 to 5 existence. The first priority is to be a good teacher and to let my students know that I am actually interested in them, and care about them. Once you build this connection, it's not as important where you teach or how much you charge. Realize your students are unique individuals, and work in the music they want to play. Most people don't want to be a virtuoso, they just want to play guitar. The relationship with a teacher is something a student won't get with a computer. It's important for students to know that they have a teacher that knows what they are doing and has a passion for the guitar."

—Eric Clemenzi, Guitar/Bass Teacher
EricClemenzi.com

Why do you want to teach? Do you genuinely want to share your passion and love for music? Or are you just looking for a few extra bucks?

I suggest you get into teaching for the right reasons. Yes, you can make some extra money quickly, but not if you act like you are doing students a favor by teaching them. To be a good teacher, you really must engage and work at developing your craft.

Giving guitar lessons can be extremely rewarding, but it can also take a lot of mental energy trying to get the most out of your students. Are you up for the challenge? The relationships you develop with students, watching them become better musicians and people, are incredibly rewarding!

THE STABILITY OF A TEACHING BUSINESS

One of the really great things about teaching guitar lessons is the steady income. Playing live and studio gigs is great, but I was never able to get out of the hunter/gatherer mentality. As one gig fell through, I would have to find another one. If your teaching business is set up correctly, it is much easier to have a steady income and to grow your business accordingly.

The overhead in teaching lessons can be low, or nonexistent, as it is characterized as a "sweat equity" type of business. What's in your head is more valuable to your business's success than what is in your bank account. Many businesses (restaurants, for example) have the issue of often being hundreds of thousands of dollars in debt to the business before the doors even open. Retail businesses, for another example, have the problem of forecasting what their sales will be *day by day*, or month by month. They are guessing and hoping that the sales trends will materialize. But a music lessons business will provide you with a much more financially stable existence—if you set it up right!

The problem with a traditional job is that it is usually your only source of income. If that source disappears, the income disappears with it. However, when you give private guitar lessons, each student becomes a source of income. This can be very beneficial to long-term planning in the growth of your business, and to being able to plan your life and your finances.

Can You Make a Living Teaching?

Many musicians discount the idea of teaching guitar lessons for a living. They are restrained by the idea that the teaching profession is a poor man's way of scraping by. I disagree. This isn't the public school system, after all. As creative and artistic activities are being phased out of schools, smart people realize the benefits of music education and are willing to pay private entities to provide those benefits.

Let's run some numbers.

Assume that you can build a student base of thirty hours a week. This would have you working from 3:00 to 9:00, Monday through Friday. Say you are charging $50 per hour. That would give you (gross):

- a weekly pay of about $1,500
- a monthly pay of about $6,500
- a yearly pay of about $78,000

Many people are blown away when they see these numbers, which are well over the national average salary for working *less* than forty hours! It is certainly above the average teacher's salary. And you could easily *do more.* Even if you did lessons for thirty to forty hours week, you would still have plenty of time for gigs and such.

Remember, there are people who value the service of music lessons. Our job is to find them!

SELF-ASSESSING

Before you begin teaching guitar lessons, you need to assess yourself as a musician. What do you have to offer as a teacher? What are your strong points? What are your weaknesses? How can you minimize your weak points as a teacher and still be effective? Many musicians sell themselves short in this area. Remember that the majority of students you teach will be beginners or intermediate players. Many would-be teachers disqualify themselves because they feel they need to be master players to accommodate beginner students. This is almost never the case. What is much more important is the ability to convey and communicate what you know to another person. You likely won't start off with many advanced-level students. I find it much more fulfilling to take beginner or intermediate students and turn them into advanced students.

If you are not great at learning songs on the fly or coming up with new ideas, lesson planning can help you tremendously. This puts your student in a certain direction and keeps you ahead of the game. I once shadowed a guitar teacher who was not a great player by any stretch of the imagination. However, he was very effective because he structured his lessons around what he was good at and presented that to the students as what they were going to learn that day. It worked.

My recommendation is this: Try to find what motivates the student to want to play, consider what you can best offer, and then structure your lesson around that. For beginner and intermediate students' lessons, the most critical elements in their success are the personal connections you make with the students and their comfort level with your ability to deliver quality instruction. For example, if you have good ears, you might be able to figure out the songs that students bring in pretty quickly. You can then enrich the lesson style by presenting theory, scales, and other musical concepts as they relate to that song. Customizing the lessons to the students' interests like this also makes the concepts stick.

It's important that you find what you are good at and maximize that. For the areas where you are deficient, work toward getting better. As a guitarist, I realized my fingerstyle playing was not up to snuff. Knowing that many students were interested in finger picking and would be asking for this, I spent some extra time developing my own technique. Once you know it, you can teach it forever. The time invested in learning craft is well worth it.

Take some time and self-evaluate. If it is your personality to teach out of a guitar book, then by all means, use that in your lessons. However, being in touch with your students' current interests is vital.

TEACHING AT HOME VS. AT A DEDICATED COMMERCIAL STUDIO

Where you teach is something you should give a lot of thought. Many people who teach at home are reluctant to even think about getting a dedicated teaching space. Let's look at some of the advantages of teaching at home.

Advantages of a Home Studio

- Little or no overhead
- No need to buy many duplicate items for your studio
- No commute time to and from work
- Savings on gas

Disadvantages of a Home Studio

- Zoning restrictions. Your space probably isn't zoned for doing lessons. Unless you want to attract unwanted attention for the amount of people going in and out of your place, having lots of traffic isn't good.
- Insufficient parking
- Insufficient insurance. If someone is hurt on your property it could be bad, bad news. You can get a bigger policy at home, but this could put you in harm's way if you do not have an official home-based business.
- Invasion of privacy to your home. How do the people you share your space with feel about having lessons in their home?
- Pets that students might not want to contend with. Also, do you have animals that don't want to contend with your students? (ha ha)
- Your house being constantly set up for business.

One of the issues I experienced, when I used to give lessons in my home, was always feeling like I was at work, as my teaching space was the same as my living space. Having a commercial space made it easier to focus on doing the lessons and spending time maintaining and growing my business. Do not underestimate the value of this.

Advantages of a Commercial Space

- The business is perceived as a real business and gives you more credibility.
- You have the ability to improve the quality of your business, and the lesson experience.
- A commercial location will usually be in a more convenient location.
- A commercial location will often give you the ability to advertise just by the visibility of the location. This in itself can make the place pay for itself.
- Your rent and other expenses from the space are a 100 percent tax write-off. In your home, you can only deduct the space if you only use it for your business, 100 percent of the time.
- Higher tuition is perceived as justified.

Disadvantages of a Commercial Space

- You must sign a lease for the space. It can be scary to know that you will spend a long amount of time paying for a space that you are unsure if you can fill. This is a commitment not to be taken lightly, as a breach can be very expensive and land you in court. We will talk about how to get lease-savvy later in this book.
- "The two of everything syndrome." You may have to buy many duplicate items for your studio.
- It feels more like a business. There will be extra expenses for this: utilities, insurance, and extra supplies. But all of them are write-offs, and heating and cooling a small teaching space is relatively inexpensive.

Providing In-Home Lessons

Many teachers provide lessons in the students' homes. This can be a good thing, depending on where you are located. In-home lessons can also be beneficial in a market where no other studio or teacher offers that service. The time a family can save not having to drive their kids back and forth can be invaluable. Remember to offer this as a premium service and charge accordingly. I would say, marking up your normal lessons rate by 20 to 25 percent would be a good place to start. One downside to this is that you will often be tying up your prime teaching hours (afternoons) driving to these lessons. You also need to determine how far you have to drive to give them.

The prime times of teaching lessons are weekday nights, so be careful limiting your availability by doing in-house lessons during those times. The upside to teaching at a student's home is that you can offer lessons without having to rent a studio or use your house. A downside is that the quality of instruction will be lowered by the student being distracted in their own home. A reliable car is a must, here.

Teaching in a Music Store

One variation to teaching at home or in a commercial space is teaching in someone else's commercial space. Many music stores provide space for teachers to teach on the premises. Usually in this scenario, the teacher pays a rental fee to use the space, while the store books the students. The store has eliminated you as being classified as an employee by renting you the space, so you are still running your own business. This scenario can be good for teachers that hate promoting themselves and just want to teach and show up to work. It can be a good way to develop your business, as most teachers work in more than one studio or location. They may teach one day at home, three days at someone else's studio, another day at a music store, etc.

What Do I Recommend?

If you can, I recommend to most teachers that they start teaching at home. You can learn your trade and begin to anticipate cycles and plan accordingly. Teachers often underestimate when it is time to stop doing home-based lessons, and subsequently miss out on the growth and upside of expanding into a commercial location.

Relocating to a commercial site was one of the best moves I made to help my business to grow.

A couple of variations on the idea of getting your own commercial space could be sharing space with an established teacher, or subletting space from a working professional and teaching during their "off hours." Many self-employed teachers work 9 to 5 with weekends off, which runs counter to when most people want music lessons. I have known people to be successful in both of these situations, so do what works for you!

There could also be opportunities to rent space at schools, churches, libraries, or community centers. Keep your eyes open for any of these opportunities!

SETTING UP YOUR BUSINESS

Pricing Strategy

How do you price yourself? The biggest mistake I see teachers make consistently is *under* charging for their services. When you are pricing your lessons, research your market, and access the strengths and weaknesses of each competitor. Try to figure out what your potential students are really paying for. Some things to consider:

Are you a university graduate?

This can establish credibility immediately with potential students, as many of your competitors aren't graduates. Many teachers haven't studied music anywhere at all. I am very aware that this credential does not automatically mean that you can teach, or that you are even qualified on your instrument, but that's how degrees are perceived in the marketplace. Not having a degree will factor into your pricing but can be overcome by factors such as being a well-known performer in your area.

I recommend looking closely at your strengths and weaknesses. Compare them with your competition and then maximize your benefits. You may have a great personality that just connects with people, or are such a great player that people are drawn to you.

Do you have a graduate degree?

A graduate degree is a nice credential to have, but I don't feel it pushes you into a different price range for private lessons. It does make you more attractive to teach in colleges as an adjunct or faculty member. Is there a teaching component to your degree (PhD, masters of education, etc.)? This is something that can enhance your qualifications to teach and broadens the interest level of potential students.

Do you have a name as a performer? Are you a local celebrity?

If you are well known as a performer, many people won't care about your educational background, but will be sold on your abilities as a player. Your name alone could be a draw.

Do you teach from home or in a studio?

For many people, teaching in a commercial studio means that you are teaching in a more professional environment, and the expectation of higher tuition comes with it. Teaching lessons from your home usually commands less money, *unless* you have a big enough name as a teacher or performer.

What area of town do you live in?

Are you teaching in the nice area of town? Shady area of town? Live in a not-so-great neighborhood? How is the parking? How accessible are you to highways and major roads? What is there to do while parents are waiting for their child's lessons? Convenience is gigantic to people as is how they perceive the ease of finding you. This can be critical.

What else can you offer?

Bass lessons, banjo, ukulele, dobro? If you can't play these well, it may be worth your time to learn. These niche instruments are in demand and can fill spots quickly.

If you do not play the uke, I recommend learning it. It is a very simple instrument to play, and it is enjoying a resurgence. Many students view this instrument as an easy way to get started playing music, and I often recommend it to parents who have students in the five- to six-year-old range, who are too young to play the guitar. As always, the more services you can offer, the more you can work.

Can you teach theory?

Songwriting? Arranging? Technology or recording?

The most important theme in your pricing structure is being able to justify the value. Some people argue that just throwing up a high price automatically means you are a great teacher. You may sway some people with this approach, but I think it's important that in a business, you walk it like you talk it. Your price should be the part of the whole picture—how your website looks, how your advertising looks, your location, how your studio looks, and so on. This idea alone can be a revelation to many people.

Naming Your Studio

When you are setting your business, here are a few things to think about if you plan to give your studio a name.

Are you building a business, or are you building a trade? If your idea is to eventually bring other teachers in, or to ever entertain the idea of selling your business, you may want to give your business a name, separate from your own. Changing later can be difficult. For example, "Overstock.com" is now "O.Co." I have seen some really horrendous names for businesses, so give this a lot of thought. Your business name should be:

- Easy to remember
- Almost impossible to mispronounce
- Almost impossible to misspell
- URL (website address) is available with the premium .com listing
- The name is available with your state's Secretary of State.

My studio, North Main Music, is located in Nashua, New Hampshire, which is known as the "Gate City." So naturally, there are more businesses named "Gate City Whatever" than I care to mention. I understand why people would choose to imitate the use of a term, but it is not a great way to separate ourselves from all the other businesses, especially if they are in similar trades. One of my clients remarked that he thought that name was boring, but it fit my criteria: it was easy to remember, impossible to mispronounce and misspell, and I could obtain both the URL and registration with the Secretary of State's office.

Two good ways to check the availability of a name (if you choose to use one):

- Check the Secretary of State in your state. They will have a business name lookup that will check the availability of the name that you are looking for. Even if it is available, it's not a slam-dunk that you can get it, but it's a good start.

- Confirm that the URL is available for that name, or for some useful variation on it. If your name is not available or becomes too compromised, try another name. The last thing you want is a URL that is something like www.joesguitarlessons/mac/Jonesboro/joe.com. Simple and clean is the way to go here.

Don't forget to *own* your own URL, even if you use another business name. It is valuable to own your name. I purchased MikeMcAdam.com in 1998. There is another Mike McAdam in the Nashville area that by coincidence plays guitar and has quite a few more record credits than I do. Despite this, I was able to get the URL and still own it today.

Setting up Bank Accounts

When you start your business, make sure you set up a separate checking account and a debit or credit card to use for your business. If you have a business name, you will need to set it up legally before you are allowed to use it printed on a checking account. Until your legal business entity is set up, you can use a DBA (Doing Business As) account. Having an account designated for your business makes it easier to track what you spend personally and what you spend on your business. There is nothing worse than sitting around on April 14th trying to remember if the Staples purchase you made on January 12th of the previous year was personal or business. If you haven't already, do this now, and put it on autopilot. I see many people screw themselves by not setting up dedicated accounts.

Online Accounting Programs

Once your bank accounts are set up, check out an online accounting program. These are very simple to use and will make your business life easier and more profitable. The major services are Quicken and QuickBooks. These are great, but they can be expensive and more complicated than you need. Since we are not in a business that holds inventory or sells things (Point of Sale business), your need for a fancy accounting program is unnecessary.

I really like a program called Outright. It's $10 a month and Web-based, easy to use and set up, and accessible from any computer. Outright requires no initial buy-in and there are no upgrades to maintain. It will sync up whatever bank accounts you want it to have access to, and will give P&L (Profit and Loss) statements, as well as breaking down income and expenses by categories. I spend about ten minutes (!) a month going through Outright, just checking to see that all of my expenses are categorized correctly and all the numbers are accurate. This saves a lot of valuable time, compared to doing it all on paper! Taxes will be your biggest expense, so spend the time getting this set up correctly.

Incorporating Your Business

Many people feel the need to incorporate their business sooner than later. Incorporation costs about $100 to $200 a year to maintain. I don't feel this is a necessary step if you are planning on doing lessons on your own with your own name... *at first.* Incorporation is important once you are established, as there are tax and legal benefits to doing so. Many people will use LLCs (Limited Liability Companies) for their business structure. The benefits of doing this are:

- Separating your personal income and assets from your businesses.

- Separating yourself from any liability due to legal action. Your chances of this are pretty low, even in such a litigious society, and your insurance will handle this part of it (more on this later).

- Establishing a name for your business that is separate from your own, i.e., "Super Joe's Music Lessons."

Talk to an attorney about incorporating your business. Many people will file the paperwork and do it *wrong.* Good, sound, legal advice is not cheap, but is money well spent. Ask around about attorneys. Often they will do LLC setup for a reasonable price in the hopes of getting more of your business later on. I have known people who have set up shop with template or online business formation documents and then have a real attorney fix them later. If your documents are not set up correctly, they can be blown to bits if you have to defend yourself in court. Protect yourself by keeping your business and personal finances separate.

Setting Up Your Work Space

What will you need in your studio? Much of this depends on what instrument you play and whether you are teaching in a studio or in your home. Here are some suggestions regardless of what instrument you play.

In the lessons studio:

- Metronome: One must keep time...right? Many teachers also use online drum machines or programs like Band in a Box.

- Clock: Preferably in a place where the teacher can see it at all times.
- Music Stand: One will do.
- Books: Any relevant teaching books that you may need
- Staff or tablature paper
- Assignment paper: I have a pile of blank paper that I write assignments or other notes on for students.
- Tuner: If this pertains to your instrument.
- Chairs: A comfortable chair for your student is key. Remember, you may be sitting for long periods of time so a good chair is a good investment for you too.
- Copier: There are now many inexpensive copiers that are easy to use.
- Computer with Internet access: Even for instruments that tend to rely on books for instruction (piano for example), it's a good idea to have access to many online tools such as YouTube.
- Extra pens/pencils
- Stapler
- Extra guitar picks. You will *fly* through these.
- Extra quarter-inch cables: At least two. Cables tend to die in bunches, so you will be glad to have the extras. I buy Monster brand because they have a lifetime warranty. If there's a problem, I bring them to Guitar Center, and they replace them on the spot.
- Capo
- Extra strings: Either you or your students will need these. I suggest getting sets of just the high E and B strings, since those break the most.
- Accessories for changing strings: Wire cutters, string winders, and hex wrenches. Many students are unfamiliar with how to change strings and will be counting on you to get it done.
- Extra Guitar: This is handy if you break a string and don't have time to change it on the spot.

- iPad or iPhone: There are many devices and phones that will do the same things. The ability to record sound and video clips for lessons on the fly is very valuable.
- Playback Device: Your phone, iPad, iPod, laptop, CPU, or boom box can work for this.
- Two Amplifiers: For students, I recommend a low cost but decent amp. I like using modeling amps for students, as they are inexpensive and cover a wide variety of sounds. And they don't burn through tubes!

Software/Apps/Technologies that Enhance Lessons

I am a big fan of anything that makes the lesson experience better for the student. There are certain tools I use to enhance my lessons. While these tools are helpful, they are not "doing the lesson for me." I use the program Guitar Pro, and while I think it is a great program, many students have erroneously felt that just using that program will do the job. It is just a tool, and only as good as the quality of the transcriptions that get programmed into it. Guitar Pro plays MIDI arrangements of primarily guitar-driven music. It also has some value as a notation creator and editor. Guitar Pro also allows you to loop sections of songs and change the pitch and tempo. Many people complain about the MIDI generated stiffness of the tracks, but again, it is just a tool. Practice with the real recordings!

- GarageBand. I love GarageBand. I think it is super cool, because it's a great combination of ease of use and power. Programs like this are a microcosm of what is great about music. Students can very easily get started making noises and learning production basics. This alone can make your job much easier, as once students get into this, they can get addicted! GarageBand is currently available for *free* on Mac computers and is a mere $3.99 for the iPhone and iPad app. Many people will also use programs like Audacity, which is another free, easy-to-use recording program.

- Song Surgeon. There are many similar programs out there, but I have been using this one. Sound Surgeon is like a super-powered version of Media Player. It allows you to slow down sections, loop sections, and change the tuning or pitch on the fly. This is great when students are confronted with challenging bits of pieces. There is an upgraded version that allows you to work with video. This is helpful, as I am increasingly working with YouTube videos that students bring into their lessons.

- Band-in-a-Box. This program has been around forever! Despite this, I still find it very useful for coming up with laser quick arrangements. Like Guitar Pro, it is only as good as its MIDI-generated, pre-programmed computer sounds can be, but it's great for student use.

- Guitar Pro. Again, Guitar Pro is a popular notation/tab program that has access to hundreds of thousands of songs, scale exercises, warm-ups, etc. The quality of these varies, but there are many good files out there.

In Your Common/Waiting Area

Create a seating area that people can exist in for up to an hour every week. I once saw a waiting area that had beanbag chairs in their waiting area—not very comfortable! While you don't have to spend a fortune, try to get decent furniture that will last. Craigslist or office supply warehouses are a good place to start. You can also find decent furniture at Target. That is, if you don't already have extra items lying around. Spend a half hour in whatever chairs you use, and find out how comfortable they really are.

- Clock

- Radio or TV? This is your call. Some teachers like having their lessons be heard. Some hate it. Think about it.

- Reading materials: Coffee-table type books tend to be more popular than magazines and are nice to have around. Many people seem to be more than entertained while on their phone or tablet devices.

- Wi-Fi access: I will repeat: many people seem to be more than entertained while on their phone or tablet devices. This is a must-have. You will most likely be using the Internet for your lessons, as well.

- Bathroom access: Part of the stress of doing lessons in your home is that you have to work harder to keep the common areas of your home clean at all times.

The main point here is to work with what you have. I have seen teachers come up with inspiring, cool workspaces in a variety of styles and budgets. If you want a clean, professional look, do that. If you want your space to be bold and have lots of color, go with it.

CHAPTER 1 TAKEAWAYS
- Spend time accessing your skills sets.
- Where do you want to teach? Many teachers work in more than one location.
- Get the basics of your business set up before you start advertising your lessons.

CHAPTER 2

Setting Your Policies

"Being a good player is a given, but you have to stick around to be really successful. I've found that diversity helps, as well as being able to work with a wide variety of personalities. You have to sometimes be a therapist and a teacher at the same time. It's rewarding to see that you can have a big impact on a student. Sometimes, students assume it's easy, but there is a lot of administrative work and lesson planning that goes on outside of the actual lesson. This all leads up to making the lesson an experience for the student.

The funniest question I've been asked by a student was, 'What do you do for a regular job?' Sometimes, people need to be reminded that this is what we do to pay the bills."

—Eric Puslys, Guitar Teacher

DEVELOPING POLICIES

Studying other studios and talking to other teachers is essential to setting up your studio policies. Find out what works for them and why they chose their own particular policies. Even after you have established your studio, continue getting other teachers to discuss their policies and procedures. This will help you to refine your own policies, and will help you to communicate as clearly and to the point as possible. It is of critical importance that you clearly define what your policies are and understand why you abide by them. Eliminate what does not work, and amplify what does!

Spend the necessary amount of time working on and perfecting your studio policies. This is the manifesto of your studio. Much of your success will be won or lost here.

Our official policy sheet is shown in figure 2.1.

North Main Music Policies

Lesson Tuition

$125 per month for weekly 30 minute lessons

$185 per month for weekly 45 minute lessons

$235 per month for weekly 60 minute lessons

Payment Policy

North Main Music uses automatic withdrawals for lesson payments. We do not accept cash or checks except for trial lessons. You can use your checking account, debit card, or credit card for monthly payment. The withdrawal takes place on the first of every month, which prepays lessons through the end of that month. Tuition is non-refundable. There is a $20 fee for non-sufficient funds.

Make-Up Lesson Policies

In the event where a student is absent, we do not offer mandatory makeup lessons. Missed lessons will be offered if the instructor has an available timeslot that week. If the lesson is missed and not made up, it is forfeited and will not be credited or made up in the future.

North Main Music does offer makeup lessons should a session be missed by the instructor, cancelled due to holidays, or inclement weather. In the event where the student is either vacationing or observing a religious holiday, a makeup is offered if North Main Music is notified at least seven days in advance.

North Main Music is closed for the following annual holidays: New Year's Day, Memorial Day, Independence Day, Thanksgiving, and Christmas Day. We also close at 6:00 p.m. on Christmas Eve Day and New Year's Eve Day.

Vacations

If a student will be missing a lesson due to being on vacation, a makeup lesson will be offered provided that North Main Music is given a seven-day prior notice. If a student takes an extended vacation you may stop automatic payment withdrawal by providing a thirty-day notice. Please note that if a student takes an extended leave of absence, North Main Music cannot guarantee that the student's spot on our schedule will be available upon return.

Discontinuing Lessons

A thirty-day notice is required to vacate lessons so that we can cancel your auto withdrawal payment.

Contact Information

North Main Music can be reached at 603-505-4282, or at NorthMainMusic@gmail.com.

We are happy to have you with us.

Enjoy your learning experience here at North Main Music!

FIG. 2.1. North Main Music Official Policy Sheet

Let's do some explaining....

At North Main Music, we have a signup sheet. The signup sheet gathers each customer's payment and contact information. This sheet also lays out our general policies (figure 2.1) and answers most questions that students and parents have about their lessons. Let's look at each dimension of our policy sheet.

TUITION

I highly recommend using an auto-pay system for receiving tuition payments, which automatically transfers the lesson amount from the client's account to yours. Even if you do not use an auto-pay system, it would be wise to make your lesson rate the same every month, regardless of whether there are four or five weeks in a month. Why? It's much easier for a person to absorb the cost of lessons as a onetime monthly fee, and see it as a reoccurring fee, than to have to try to figure out whether there are four or five weeks in a month of lessons. When I first opened my lessons studio, I started out charging tuition fees by the number of lesson weeks in a month. We would invoice students toward the end of the month for the upcoming month. Even if it was a five-week month, many people would erroneously write a check for just four weeks of lessons. Then I would either have to ask the student, or the student's parent, for the additional payment at the next lesson, which was uncomfortable. Or, I would have to call and ask to be paid and hopefully get it the next week. This is a loser's game.

This type of system might work if you only have a handful of students and you have lots of free time to spend trying to collect money owed to you. The most important point is you want a tuition plan that is scalable and will work whether you have one student or a hundred.

After carefully researching the competition in our area, we set our tuition rate at $27 per half hour lesson. To get our monthly tuition, we multiplied $27 by 52 (weeks) and divided it by 12 (months). A method I recommend, no matter what rate you use. At North Main Music, we offer a tuition reduction for families that register multiple members for lessons. A rate reduction is also given to students who decide to take a longer length lesson

(45 or 60 minutes). In my experience, I don't find tuition reduction to be a big incentive for people to upgrade to a longer lesson time, as they usually will want to for reasons other than financial considerations.

After years of chasing overdue tuition payments, I suggest getting *prepaid* for the entire month of lessons. This locks the person in for the month and allows you to pay your bills on time as well. I have known many teachers who allow students to pay by the week, and this can become problematic. When people are not invested financially in their lessons, many of them are not committed beyond the lesson they just paid for. You will wind up losing your shirt when students disappear without calling to cancel their lesson. Or, when they decide to leave out a lesson payment from their tuition check because they don't see the necessity in paying for a lesson they skipped out on. In my studio, the way around this is to flat-line the lesson rate: $125 a month for half an hour lessons (or whatever rate you choose).

Payment Policy

The payment policy you choose is vital to the health and welfare of your business, so invest the time necessary to get it right. I have talked to many studio owners who have done a great job enrolling students and are on track to financial success, but then run into problems with two things: how they get paid, and their makeup policies.

Our Auto-Pay Sheet

Figure 2.2 is North Main Music's current auto-pay sheet. We present this form to students on their first day to fill out, and it contains much of the information that you will need to process their payments. Your own form will be dictated in part by what your merchant payment company will ask you to provide as proof that you are running things above board when collecting information from clients.

NORTH MAIN MUSIC

REGISTRATION FORM/AUTOMATIC PAYMENT CONSENT FORM

Last Name:_____ Parent's Name:_____

Student Name(s)		
Student Birthdate(s)		
Medical Conditions	☐ No ☐ Yes	☐ No ☐ Yes
Instrument/Class		
Lesson Day/Time		
Lesson Length	☐ 30 min ☐ 45 min ☐ 1 hr	☐ 30 min ☐ 45 min ☐ 1 hr
Date Starting Lessons	DD/MM/YY	DD/MM/YY

Phone #:_____ Work/Cell Phone #:_____

Address:_____
            Street   City   Postal Code

Where did you hear about us?_____

Email Address:_____

☐ Referral:_____   ☐ Other:_____

Date Registered:_____
                            Day   Month   Year

Method of Payment

*All charges will appear on your bank or credit card statement as North Main Music Checking Account. Attach void check here.

☐ Visa ☐ Master Card:_____ Expiration Date:_____
                                        Card Number
☐ Discover

Card Holder's Name:_____

Checking Account Information:

Routing No:_____Checking Account No:_____

I hereby authorize North Main Music to charge my account the amount of

$_____ on the first day of each month starting _____

I will give the school office one month's written notice from the first of the month to discontinue these charges. I understand the school policies on the back of this page and agree to abide by them.

_____   _____
Signature   Date

FIG. 2.2. North Main Music Auto-Pay Sheet

A couple of notes about that sheet

When getting phone numbers, we ask people to give us the phone number by which it is easiest to reach them. Sometimes, people give us their house phone numbers (remember those?), which they *never* check for messages.

We also ask our clients to share how they heard about North Main Music. This is critical to see where your marketing efforts are paying off. If they work, keep using them!

Payment Gateways

There are many payment gateway services you can use to set up an automatic payment system. Run an Internet search, and shop around for a service that will best suit your particular needs. For most payment gateways, you will need to present yourself as an established business, with business checking accounts, and an Employer Identification Number (EIN), which you can receive in minutes after filling out the online application at IRS.gov. In some cases, you might need a commercial "brick and mortar" location.

A very easy auto-pay system to start with is PayPal. PayPal allows you to set up shop very easily and quickly, and although they are not the most inexpensive option, it usually breaks down to about 3 percent per transaction. Simplifying your payment system and receiving your tuition fees in a timely manner makes this small transaction fee well worth the investment. With an auto-pay system in place, your business can deduct tuition on the first of the month, and the funds will be available in your account in two to four business days.

I personally like PayPal because it has great name recognition. Most people already have an established account, so they feel comfortable sharing their account information with you. Even if the perception is that musicians are flaky and freaky, people feel secure setting up a reoccurring payment plan using PayPal's service.

If I had continued to run our tuition collection the old way, collecting paper checks, my business would have failed a long time ago. Why? Because at the beginning of every month, I would be scrambling to cover my overhead shortages from late tuition payments with early tuition payments for the current month. This is the business equivalent of robbing Peter to pay Paul.

When students or their parents ask, "Can I just pay by check?" I tell them that we really aren't set up to process checks, and that having an auto-pay system in place actually makes everything easier for our students and parents. Whatever their objection is, make sure you emphasize what a time saver and what a stress reliever it will be for them: no more having to remember to bring the checkbook to write a check! I once had a client tell me, "Well, I'm not sure I'm going to have the money every month!" Obviously, he had bigger problems to deal with than paying for his guitar lessons! People will also ask about paying with cash. You know the expression "Cash is king," so you will have to make this call depending on your own particular situation. My observation has been that most people who insist on paying with cash wind up being pretty reliable.

Another giant benefit to an auto-pay system is the amount of time saved doing paperwork. Printing invoices, cashing checks, notating who has paid and who hasn't, calling people about bounced checks, and calling people who paid the wrong amount can be a tremendous waste of your valuable time. By establishing an auto-pay system, I started saving an average of *five* hours a month. What a relief!

Another alternative that is becoming popular is a card swiper that you can use on your phone or tablet. This is an easy way to get paid, and you can use this if you decide to add books or accessories sales to your business. PayPal, Square, and many national banks are examples of companies that offer this service. You need to prove that you are a legit business before you can get one of these POS (Point of sale) terminals.

PayPal also has a service that allows people to agree to have you withdraw from their account every month. This can be another alternative to help you get paid on time.

Tracking Who Has Paid

Even if you are using an auto-pay system, you want to verify that each payment has been made. If you are not using such a system, you still want to keep track of who has paid and who hasn't. When I used to take checks, I made scans of the checks just to make sure.

VACATIONS

One of the tremendous advantages to having an auto-pay system is the ability to avoid losing income when families take vacations. When people pay you at the beginning of the month (especially if it is automated), they are not likely to think about the vacations they are taking in February and April (which inconveniently occur at the end of the month). Auto-pay will give you much more flexibility in being able to schedule a makeup time and avoid losing money for lessons lost to vacation absences.

MAKEUP LESSON POLICY

Once you've established your tuition policy, the next most important system to spend some time considering is your makeup lesson policy. If you do not define and clearly articulate your makeup policy, you will soon have the inmates running the asylum. It's important to immediately establish a student's commitment to the time that they have signed up for. Many people giving lessons will allow a student to make up a lesson "whenever," however many times the student wants. Many will also allow people to cancel within twenty-four hours of the lesson and then offer the student a makeup time! In my experience, the more black and white our makeup polices are, the more people follow them. With most people, you will only have to have this conversation once when you first meet them, and then restate your makeup lesson policies in writing. It is only a small percentage of people that will challenge you on this. Again, having an auto-pay type setup (where they have prepaid for the month) will give you leverage.

At North Main Music, our policy is that a makeup lesson will be offered the week of the missed lesson, if it is available. If there is no other spot available, that particular lesson is forfeited. This keeps attendance up (good for you) and prevents the phone call ten minutes before a lesson that goes something like this: "We won't make it back in time from the beach.... Can we have a makeup?!"

When scheduling makeups, don't be afraid to offer hours when you are available and when you *aren't*. Teachers who aren't firm about scheduling times can find themselves doing makeup lessons on Sunday at 12:30 because they feel badly telling the student they are not available that day/time. One good way to avoid this is to leave a small time open in your schedule every week just for makeup lesson opportunities.

Exceptions to this are when students have vacations or other dates that you know about with advance notice. These situations are easy to deal with and will give you the opportunity to avoid having to deduct the lesson, if dealt with proactively.

Another exception I will make is weather. Here in New England, we have a four-season climate with plenty of snow. Some people will not drive if one flake hits the ground; others will drive through a blizzard. I tend to be more liberal about people missing lessons due to bad weather conditions because, again, our students are prepaid and they will be much more accommodating in making the lesson up. Without an auto-pay system, snow days (not uncommon here) can be very expensive, especially when there are four weeks in a month. Having the lessons prepaid gives you the opportunity to make your income much more stable, and you will not lose income as a result of missed lessons.

Whatever you do, have a clear policy that you stick to.

HOLIDAYS

We are closed for major holidays. We are open for all of the "Monday Holidays." This is your call, but in my experience, I find that most people will come in for their lesson. You can easily reschedule those who don't.

DISCONTINUING LESSONS

One drawback of an auto-pay system is that you will have students that will call you on the 4th or 5th of the month to cancel or withdraw from lessons. "Hi. We've decided to pull Johnny from lessons immediately. Can we have a refund?" To avoid this, I ask, in writing, that people give us a thirty-day notice before they discontinue lessons. Be clear on this in your contracts from the beginning, and it will minimize trouble.

You can make exceptions for this, but remember that this policy is in place to protect you. Before North Main Music instituted an auto-pay system, I would get what I called, "The incredible disappearing student syndrome." It works like this:

Jane's lesson starts on the 6th of the month. Jane does not show up, and Jane does not call. Jane has told everyone but you (her teacher) that she has quit music lessons. Jane has no reason to call you, because she won't have to pay you anymore for lessons if she doesn't see you again. Sounds cynical, but it happens a lot. This can get expensive quickly, and students stopping lessons tends to come in waves. Protecting yourself with an auto-pay system can minimize this problem, if not eliminate it altogether. It's amazing how proactively people handle their lives when *their* money is involved.

CHAPTER 2 TAKEAWAYS

• Payment and makeup policies are the two most important policies you have.

• Create a well thought out, scalable policy that addresses those major issues.

CHAPTER 3

Marketing Materials

"People think that success happens overnight, but it takes patience and a lot of organized effort. Some people will ask themselves whether teaching is worth sticking with, but a great teacher is a coach that can be a guide and a resource to a student. Teaching one-on-one can be draining, so I feel it's important to give 100 percent and give that student the best experience. Creating my own method books of guitar teaching has laid out a plan of working a student toward a specific goal. In my studio, I have a list of ten ways a student can get the best out of their playing."
—Greg Arney, Founder of Boston Guitar Lessons
BostonGuitarLessons.net

BUSINESS GOALS

When you are developing your business's marketing approach, it is important to consider your overall goals. Some of the suggestions in this chapter will take time and considerable effort to accomplish. It is important to set goals and to determine what the biggest impact items are, and the order in which they need to occur. What combination of small goals unlocks the big goal? What is the process? Many people get caught up on small details that lead them into dead ends and take away from the biggest impact items.

To keep your goals prioritized and on schedule, I suggest writing a business plan. A business plan is a document that states what your intentions are, the timeline you have set for your goals, and the order in which they need to be achieved. This sort of roadmap can keep you on course as you work toward the ultimate goal of filling your lessons schedule, and clarifying your ideas before you begin your marketing outreach will help you get the right message across.

TRADING SERVICES

If you are operating on a budget (and who isn't?), it's important to use your resources wisely. I am a big fan of trading services. Many people waste valuable time and money trying to DIY everything in their business. I have seen more amateurish-looking business cards and websites because people were too cheap, or not resourceful enough, to find a creative alternative to doing it themselves. Assess your strengths, and use them accordingly. If you are good at graphics, then do the design work yourself. If you aren't good at designing websites or graphics, find someone who is.

Early on, I did some handouts of some musical exercises that I use every day in my lessons. While I learned a lot, I later had them redone by a real graphic artist. It took him half as much time, and the results were twice as good. Look at your existing student base and your friends, and see if any of them work in fields such as:

- Graphic Design: For flyers, business cards, other handouts
- SEO (Search Engine Optimization): You have a website. So what? How do potential students find you?
- Website Design: Web guys are becoming as specialized as doctors. Be careful of one person that says he can do it all.
- Photographer: You will need pictures for your site and promotional materials. Your iPhone probably won't cut it.
- Video: Videos are good for your website, too. Again, the Flip Video (remember those?) probably won't get it done.

If there aren't people in your social circle who can help you, you can advertise on sites such as Craigslist that you are willing to trade services for any help in these areas. Another alternative is to check out sites such as Elance.com or Odesk.com. These sites allow you to post a job description that you need (business card design, etc.) and let designers from all over the world bid on the job. You have the opportunity to go through the portfolio of the person bidding for the job and see if they have the right stuff for your job. These services are often less money than you would think. I have used both of these and had success. Much of the graphic design for my book *Absolute Beginner Guitar* was done by a designer I had found through Elance.

MARKETING MATERIALS TO GET STARTED

Flyers

Flyers are an inexpensive and effective way to get your message out there. Flyers work because they can be placed in many locations and can be seen by many people.

Figure 3.1 is our current ad.

FIG. 3.1. North Main Music Flyer

Here are some points to emphasize:

- *What do you offer?* Music lessons! This is stated in the headline but also reinforced visually. You can see this ad twenty or so feet away and get a good idea of what is being offered.
- *What separates you from the other music studios?* Think of what makes you unique or special. That's the purpose of our subtitle and the bullets at the bottom.
- *Where are you located?* Make sure your address is prominent.
- *How do I contact you?* Your phone number and website address are key information.
- I like a *lead-in line* that encourages people to go to the website: Video content is something I find works well here.
- *Tear-offs*: A tear-off (at the bottom) should include: Who you are, website, and phone number. Don't forget to add a QR code that people can scan on their smartphone and take directly to your website. Bing provides these for free. (Figure 3.1 is an 11 x 17 ad that we ran without tear-offs.)

Make your flyer stand out with a unique twist. Using different colors shapes or sizes helps to make your ad stand out. How does it look? How does it feel? Try to make it as appealing as possible. There is a guitar teacher in New York City named Dan Smith who, for years, has been running his guerilla ad campaign, "Dan Smith Will Teach You Guitar." Dan's ads have been so celebrated that there is even a parody featured on YouTube. Now, that's really great, free, publicity! Here is our version of this ad: It is a 3 x 9 ad, which is an unusual size, but effective in places you would normally see business cards.

FIG. 3.2. North Main Music Ad

Craigslist Ad

Craigslist is an effective and free way to advertise your studio. It's relatively painless to create an HTML template that can be used to make your Craiglist ad more interesting. You can flood Craigslist daily with ads using multiple email addresses; just be sure to use slight variations in your text. You can also post different ads, if you are in an area that borders several Craigslist regions. Your Craigslist ad can be a hybrid of your homepage and flyer. Study other people's ads on Craiglist well. You can learn many things by doing this:

- Your competitors' positioning angle: Are they undercutting your price? What is unique about their guitar lessons?
- Where are they located?
- What is their background and experience?

Business Cards

Business cards are a powerful, inexpensive, and easy way to get your message out into the world. Many people use free business cards from places like Vistaprint.com. With these, it is easy to find a musical theme template and create your own cards in minutes. I usually pass on the "FREE" cards that they offer as they are usually of lesser quality and have the print company's ad placed on the back. It is relatively inexpensive to get higher quality business cards, at Vistaprint or other services, and they go a long way in representing your business in a positive way. You should ultimately have your own custom business card created by a graphic designer. Print them in reasonably small quantities (to start), as you may find yourself experimenting with, or changing them often.

Here is our current business card:

FIG. 3.3. North Main Music Business Card (Front)

Information to put on your card

There are many ways to get attention with your business card. Make note of any cards that you like, and don't be afraid to incorporate elements that you think will work. At the very least, include this information:

- Who are you? North Main Music
- What are you offering? "Music Lessons for All Ages"
- Where are you located? Address
- How do I contact you? Phone and Web address

I also like the idea of having a visual representation of what you offer. In our case, the instruments speak for themselves.

One thing that is becoming popular is using the entire business card, front and back, to get your message across. Adding content to the back reinforces your message, with little or no added cost.

Serving the Nashua, Hollis &
Merrimack New Hampshire Areas   NORTH MAIN MUSIC

GUITAR - PIANO - DRUMS - VOCALS

www.NorthMainMusic.com

FIG. 3.4. North Main Music Business Card (Back)

Keep your card consistent with your other marketing materials in terms of color and style. You may find good template cards that will serve your needs.

WEBSITE

Not long ago, we were still primarily using the Yellow Pages to find everything. The Web has changed the methods people use to obtain information and find businesses. It is amazing how much websites have changed, even in the last couple of years, and they will probably change again in a couple more years. Rather than try to describe the latest trends, I will present some of the basic principles that will help get your website effectively promoting and informing people about your services.

Here is our homepage:

FIG. 3.5. Home Page for North Main Music's Website

Questions that Must Be Answered on Your Site

- *What do you offer?* Describe what your business offers. This is not the place for what you personally have accomplished as a musician. Do you offer piano lessons? Guitar lessons? Are they for beginners? Kids?

- *What is in it for me?* What is the benefit of taking lessons? Will it make me smarter? Will it make me more handsome? Explain the benefits. Talk up what you offer.

- *What do I do next?* Okay, I'm sold. What do I do next? This is where your "Call to Action" should be, like, Call now to book for the summer!

- *How do I contact you?* I get frustrated when I see a site that I like and find that I am looking all over the place to find the simple contact information. Our email, phone and physical address are at the bottom of every page.

- *How much?* You don't have to have your rates right on the front of your home page, but make sure they are clearly stated. You will be amazed how many times you are asked this even though the person is right on your website.

- *Okay... Who are you?* Now is the time to talk about your qualifications and why you (and your staff, if you hire other teachers, someday) and your studio are the best choice for lessons.

- *Testimonials.* Do people have good things to say about you? Share it here. I find testimonials to be more effective when they are sprinkled over an entire site rather than an entire page dedicated to them.

Other Important Items to Include

- *Photos.* Preferably, of you teaching. Get your students or friends to help you; they can even be in the pictures. Some people are hams, some people hate cameras. Find the hams and ask them to take some photos that you can use for your site. If you don't have students yet, you can take photos of yourself playing or of your studio. You can also use stock photos, but I think they are a lot less visually appealing.

- *Videos.* Videos are a quick and easy way to get you and your program out there. Whether it's a simple video or a more sophisticated production, let's face it: people want to watch, not read or listen. Focus on how to make your videos as high quality as possible. Local high schools and colleges have students in video departments who are dying to get some work. If you decide to film your own videos, investing in some decent lighting can go a long way to making your videos look professional. Editing your video is easy to do on programs such as Windows Movie Maker or iMovie. I suggest featuring videos that showcase your teaching style as well as your personality. This gives people an idea of what it would be like to work with you and makes them feel more comfortable committing to lessons.

- *Where are you located?* It is easy to embed a Google map on your site that shows your exact location. You can enhance this by including pictures of the outside building.

- *What are your competitive advantages?* What puts your lessons above the rest? List them on your site.

Get together the best website that you can. Study good websites and see what works. Make note of them. You may not have the budget of some mega corporation, but you can come up with something that is decent and effective.

Err on the side of keeping your content clean and concise. Many people overdo it with text, but it's more effective to keep your focus points short and sweet. Google and other search engines will place you on their pages based largely on your content, so again, put a lot of thought into describing what you do and how you do it.

Information Not to Include on Your Site

- *Religious and political views.* Bad one here. Save them for Thanksgiving dinner with your family.

- *Compromising photos or information about what you did last weekend.* Remember, people can see and read your Facebook page too.

- *Policies. I don't think posting policies on a website is a good thing.* Remember, everything on your site makes or breaks the sale. You can present your lessons policies when you meet the student for their first lesson.

- *Online booking calendar.* Don't let people book over the phone or through email. I think it is much more effective to book lessons live; it gives you some control over when you are booking your appointments rather than letting people make Swiss cheese out of your schedule. This can also backfire when it comes to makeup lessons.

Website Just for Teaching

If you are a performer and you use your website to promote your upcoming shows, I recommend having a separate part of your website that highlights your teaching. While integrating your performance schedule can be powerful and a great way to establish your credibility, it's important that your teaching site be informative in terms of what you do as a teacher and how someone is able to set up lessons with you. Some of the things that you can advertise can include your teaching philosophy, what someone can expect in a lesson, sample video and audio, your teaching biography with teaching credentials and rates, and answers to some frequently asked questions. Once people have made up their mind to set up a lesson, then you can tell them your policies and how your studio operates.

Proofread, and then Proofread Again

When running ads or copy for business cards, or your website, it's key to check all copy spelling and all placements of non-text items before printing. Then have someone else (who is hopefully literate…) do the same thing. It is very easy to have misprints and mistakes in ads, if you are not careful.

Getting a Mobile Site

More and more people will be finding you through their phone browsers than through traditional computers. Make sure your site looks good on a phone's browser. Services such as DudaMobile (in conjunction with Google) can convert your website to look good on mobile devices. It's very easy to use, too.

How They Find You: SEO

SEO is an acronym for "Search Engine Optimization." It is the process of organizing the information in your site—the tags for each page and the way the site is set up—in order to get better search engine results. There are specialists that can help you with this, as the process continually changes according to search engines' criteria. The easiest way to begin is by having well-worded content that describes your business, what it offers, and where you reside. Track where you rank using a program like Google Analytics, as the results will frequently change. Adding new content and studying your competition will help as well.

Local Online Listings

Another effective online SEO tool is creating a local listing. Bing, Google, and Yahoo will list your business, and setup is free. Potential students can learn about your business and see photos, videos, and other information. These are the ads that will appear with maps when you do searches that highlight local results.

Pay-Per-Click Ads

Right now, Google, Bing, and Yahoo offer *pay-per-click* (PPC) ads. This can be an effective way to promote your business, but it can also be expensive and very ineffective, if not handled correctly. Many times, you can get a free coupon that will help you launch a PPC campaign.

It is difficult with PPC campaigns to figure out if what you are paying for is a reaction to your (organic) website or from the PPC results. This is another area of SEO that changes often, so we will not go into details of how to launch a PPC campaign. However, I recommend measuring twice and cutting once before using this strategy.

I haven't found Facebook ads to be effective. I ran a campaign for a couple of months and generated absolutely nothing, while Facebook reported gross exaggerations of how many people visited my site. (This was confirmed by Google analytics.) I have personally responded to ads I have seen on Facebook for products and services, so this could be something that works for you.

I don't support funding a ton of paid ads. This is not to say that they don't work. But just because it works for one type of business does not mean it will work for another. The techniques that will help you—reputation, quality of lessons, the relationships you build with students that create referrals—take time to develop. Be patient! Done correctly, these methods can create more students than you can fit in your schedule.

Google Analytics

An effective tool you can use to monitor the amount of traffic to
your site is Google's Analytics. Google Analytics will show you:

- how many times your site was visited
- how long they stayed
- what zip code they searched from
- what pages were visited

This information can be invaluable in planning how to update
your site and how to make it more effective.

Visit www.google.com/analytics/.

Last note about websites: Update often! The work doesn't end
after it's created. As your site will likely be your number one sales
tool, it is vital to update the content and constantly evaluate all the
copy and non-text items. This also helps with your search ratings.

Social Media

Social media is all the rage, so how do we harness this for our
own business? I have found that Facebook has functioned well
in serving existing students. People can go to your page, see
what's new, and be engaged by your posts. Many posts start
conversations that get people involved, like "What was your first
guitar?" I do not however, see having a Facebook page as being a
viable *alternative* to having a website. It is a nice addition that is
easy to use and gets people involved, but your website will have
a separate purpose.

Twitter is a bit different, in that the chain of people that are
following each other can grow exponentially. This can be powerful
in terms of getting your name and image in front of many people
who are connected to you through other non-musical contacts.
Twitter is growing in popularity, so a presence there is important.

At this point, I believe social media is more effective at
informing an existing student rather than enticing new ones.

CHAPTER 3 TAKEAWAYS

- Creating materials is a way to get your message to your potential students.

- The quality of these materials will go a long way towards getting the right people to call.

- A website is the easiest way to showcase who you are and what you do.

CHAPTER 4

Turning Inquiries into Students

"I have always been blessed with great teachers. It is a rare combination to be a great player and great teacher. You always want to put challenges in front of students to make them well rounded. As a teacher, it's important to be easy to work with and to be a good person. You can push students in thoughtful ways. Music teachers need to try to think beyond the obvious: What do you do that is unique and why do you fill a need. People are surprised to realize how much nonmusical stuff is a part of our jobs. It can take up a lot of time. Concrete goals keep me motivated to move forward."

—Andrew Hitz, Tuba Teacher
AndrewHitz.com

RETURN ALL PHONE CALLS!

I have booked a shocking number of students where the conversation goes like this: "Yeah, we called Studio X, but they never called back. Thanks for returning my call." People should not be surprised to get called back, but they often are. This is a classic example of picking the low-hanging fruit. Not returning phone calls is a great way to go out of business and an even better way to get a bad reputation. I once had a student that was booked on one of these calls, who wound up staying with our studio for over five years, taking a one-hour lesson a week. He also referred three other students. Common courtesy and attention to details can pay off massively. Remember that each student you book can potentially refer other students or family members to your studio. By doing something as stupid as not returning a phone call, these students will quickly be snatched up by your competition.

I try to live-answer the phone as much as possible. This is important, because people often change their minds (and you thought you were the only one with ADD), or hang up and call other studios. It is also a good idea to take notes on the phone conversation and leave a reminder to call them back, if you haven't booked them already. Sometimes, this extra call a week or so later will be the push someone needs to start lessons.

Phone Lines

I recommend using a dedicated phone line for your business. This is relatively inexpensive (about $10 a month), and it gives your studio a level of professionalism that can set you apart. There are two easy ways to do this:

- *Add another cell phone:* This is usually about $10 a month to add a line, and the phone price will vary. Some plans offer free phones, or you can use an inexpensive, basic model; you don't need a smartphone for this line. Or you can use a prepaid phone.

- *Virtual or PBX phone:* This is a live phone number that you can use to redirect to your normal phone. A PBX line allows you to create a more polished, pro-sounding voice message than the average cell phone recording. We use a company named VoiceNation. The line is $10 per month and works great. VoiceNation gives you the ability to use multiple lines and to send voicemails to email with audio playback.

- *Google Voice:* Google Voice is free. It provides an alternative phantom phone number that redirects to your phone(s). You can leave an alternative outgoing message that represents your business. Voicemail will be directed to your Gmail account and also sent via text message.

Maintaining a separate line is an easy way to keep the traffic down on your regular phone as well. Some of the calls you receive do not require you to drop everything to answer; "Hi, Cindy can't make it today, see you next week." A new student, however, is one that you need to prioritize.

Once you have decided to use an additional cell phone or PBX line, answer your phone with a professional greeting, including the business name, for example, "Brown Sound Music, this is Joe speaking." That's more professional than "Yo" or just "Joe speaking." Those don't create a good first impression and make you sound like an amateur.

DEVELOPING SALES SKILLS

Most musicians are *horrified* when I suggest developing sales skills. But remember, there is a giant difference between a sales huckster and someone that simply knows how to inform a potential student and direct them towards making a decision to become your client. Many people are uncomfortable with sales, but providing good information about what you provide pays off tremendously. Read at least a few books on sales, and find an approach that matches your temperament. If you are a super aggressive "closer," then work accordingly. If you are shy and reticent, then find out how to put your business in its best light. You don't have to be a piranha. At the very least, know your policies inside out, and be quick with answers to all common questions.

- Do you take beginners?
- How much are lessons?
- Are _____ lessons the same price as _____ lessons?
- Where are you located?
- Do you offer sibling discounts?
- What do I need to bring to the lesson to get started?
- I need help purchasing an instrument, what do you recommend?
- What ages do you start _____ lessons?
- How often do lessons meet?
- Is it the same day and time every week?
- Do you work with kids?

Some of these questions appear to be obvious, especially if someone has already found you through your website. Despite this, you will be asked these questions repeatedly, so practice your answers. Sometimes, people just like to ask questions, even if they already know the answers. You can also address this information on your website with a Frequently Asked Questions page (FAQ). Know your prices inside and out, as people will ask you repeated variations on the question of your pricing structure.

People will call, speak with you at length, and still not sign up for lessons. This is a reality. When this happens, I add them to our mailing list. In the future, they often sign up because you have kept them informed. Mailing lists are a good way to bring back old students, or to get siblings involved.

Evaluate your phone skills. What went wrong? What worked? A good rule of thumb: If you are on the phone longer than three minutes answering a battery of questions, they most likely won't sign up.

Age Brackets

In the beginning, you will likely be working with beginner students, and often, young children. As you become more established, you might get older and more advanced students.

There are three primary types of students you will see:

- Young Children: 9–12
- Teenagers: 12–17
- Adults: 35 and up.

I find college students and young adults are enrolled in lower numbers than other groups in private guitar lessons. In these three groups, you will need different ways of reaching the students and communicating with them. Over time, you will see many commonalities emerge. Even if you have to "fake it until you make it," your enthusiasm and commitment to becoming a better teacher will help you get through any rookie mistakes you may make.

Accomplished or intermediate students can be more interesting and can keep you on your toes. These students can often require more lesson planning and preparation. With these types of students, keeping them on a directed path is really critical.

Students Just Getting Ready for Auditions

Every now and then, I get calls from students who inquire about short-term lessons to get ready for these auditions. Many times, they have already failed an audition, or are just looking to sharpen their skills. Offering audition preparation as an additional service or addressing these types of students on your website or in your marketing materials is a good idea.

Remnant Students

"Remnant students" is my name for students who may sign up for just a few lessons. They may do it while on extended vacation, or just as a hobby during winter break or summer. These students can be a great way to fill up your schedule, as they will often be flexible and are willing to come in two to three times a week. For this type of student, I will break from our auto-pay setup and let them just buy a block of lessons.

DO YOU OFFER DISCOUNTS?

Sometimes, you will be asked if you offer any discounts. A reasonable question, but I think slashing your prices to make the sale to a customer that you have been talking to for thirty seconds is a *bad* idea. This cheapens the perception of your service and sets a bad precedent for the relationship you are about to get into. Remember that your service is extremely valuable, and that you are offering a tremendous value through your guitar lessons. Even if you really need the business, it's important to walk away from this type of potential client, if need be. If someone balks at your price, remind them that your pricing is competitive and that your service will be equal to it.

I have made exceptions to this rule. A student came to us from another school, and one of our teachers had worked with her. This student had autism and the teacher told me that she liked working with this student, but was concerned about the student affording our tuition. As the student was pre-qualified by one of our teachers, I made an exception. You will be confronted with similar situations, and each case requires consideration. Just don't give away the farm!

Free First Lessons

"Can I get the first lesson free?" This is another example of people trying to find a way to cheapen your service. My policy is that they can take one paid lesson with no strings attached. If they are happy, we will proceed. If not, they are free to walk away. I make an exception in offering a sibling a free lesson to get started. This is another example of someone being pre-qualified, so they are a safe bet. Chances are, they will like the lesson and want to continue.

Some teachers have success offering free lessons. If you set up the rest of your business well, I don't think this is necessary.

Offering Available Times

When people call to arrange times for lessons, it's important to give them options, but not too many. Why? "A confused mind does nothing," as they say, and it often overloads a prospect. *Never* say something like, "I'm wide open on Thursday. Pick anytime you want!" This makes you look like you are not very much in demand. You can say something like this: "I offer lessons on Monday, Tuesday, and Thursday. Do any of those days work for you?"

They will often answer with "Yes, Mondays are great." At that point, offer some times. I never offer more than three or four times. If they don't agree to any of the times you offered, simply ask them what would be their ideal time, and go from there. I have seen some people let students book themselves with an online calendar. *This is insane!* This hurts your credibility of being a booked, in-demand teacher, and it can lead to huge gaps in your schedule. If someone can only come in on an off time, make that decision. Often, a student that can only come during an "off time" (times other than the most popular, peak hours) can be very valuable, from a scheduling perspective.

Never be "always available." If people want the lessons, they will figure out a time that works.

Teachers Missing Lessons

Teachers who perform regularly run into conflicts with their lessons schedule. With this in mind, if you find that you gig regularly on a night that you have lessons, you may want to stop doing lessons on that day. It is important to respect that you have set a time with a student and that you have earned credibility by being there reliably. I have seen teachers lose many students due to a cavalier attitude about lesson times. When possible, deal with missed lessons and upcoming dates proactively so that you do not lose income, and make sure to let the student know that you value their time as well.

PEAK TIMES FOR TEACHING

I have a joke that there are only so many Tuesdays at 6:00 to go around. The peak time for students is generally weekdays from 4:30 to 7:00. Students who can come earlier or later are obviously more valuable, from a scheduling perspective. For some people, 7:00 P.M. is just too late. This is often the case with younger kids. The good news is many adults will find these later times to their liking, as getting home from work after 6:00 is common.

Saturdays

I find Saturday a good day to do lessons. The people that will take these times are often unavailable during weekday times, so it turns into a nice niche. You can easily start in the morning on Saturday and finish early. Sunday, on the other hand, is a pretty hard day to fill, in my experience.

TEACHING MULTIPLE STUDENTS SIMULTANEOUSLY

Sometimes, people ask if two friends or siblings can enroll in a class together. I have not had success with this, for the following reasons:

- one person is more talented than the other
- one person practices harder than the other
- one person is interested in different music than the other

In a short period of time, a chasm forms between the students' playing levels. This is unfair to the more advanced student, because you have to bring the lesson down to the other student's level. Most people understand this when it is explained to them.

I am willing to have the students play together when they have reached a certain level. This can be a tremendous bonding experience, especially if they are family members.

SCHEDULING

I am amazed at how busy people make themselves, these days. Understand that the lesson you give, whether to a child or an adult, is an activity sandwiched between ten other activities that day. A family's schedule runs like a train, and it's very important to keep that train on time by running your lessons on time. Remember that people are paying for your time, and it's important to respect that. There are students that will attempt to "suck your time," conversing with no regard to the student after them.

There are also students who will be upset if you start a minute late, or end a minute early. For your first student of the day, try to be ready ten to fifteen minutes before the lesson start time. Have all the lights on, your instrument ready to go, and your materials at hand. Students will quit if you are unprepared for lessons too many times. If you look at all the reasons you could lose students, some are within your control and some are not. This is one you have complete control over.

Here are a few ways to end your lessons on time:

- About thirty seconds before I intend to end a lesson, I put my instrument on its stand. This alone will often get the student's attention that the lesson is about to be over.
- I also hand them the book or paper they need with this week's assignment on it, and say something like "We'll finish this next week" or "Play up to this point for next week."
- If they aren't packing by this point, I stand up and walk toward the door, indicating with my body language that the lesson is ending.

If you have students that like to pepper you with questions, or who take forever to get packed up, leave a little extra time.

Much of the pressure of doing lessons is that you have to be "on" most of the time. Many jobs give you the ability to sloth through the daily activities and watch the clock. I think being a music teacher requires you to be legitimately engaged with the person you are giving the lesson to. People want to be inspired and be shown with enthusiasm what you are teaching. The death knell for any teacher is the day they start mailing it in. Don't fall into this trap! Careful attention to scheduling can help support your ability to stay engaged.

Tracking Appointments

There's an old fortune cookie proverb "The worst pen is better than the best memory." This can keep you on track preparing for lessons and keep students accountable for what they are assigned to work on.

Google Calendar is one example of a scheduling program that can sync between your phone and your computer. Schedules change constantly, and you will often be shuffling people around. Keeping an accurate calendar is the best way to give your brain a rest and remember what you wrote a month ago. You can also add notes on what students are currently working on.

Scheduling Breaks

Do you prefer to work without interruption? Are you the type of person that needs breaks in the middle of the day? I find that breaks almost always occur naturally from cancellations or other circumstances. If you are not comfortable with the randomness of this, schedule a break. I schedule a break between 6:00 and 6:15 to have dinner. I keep it short, as this is right at a peak time and I want to disturb the flow of lessons as little as possible. Having pre-prepared (brown bag) meals helps. It's important to keep your energy up, so give this some thought.

Switching Lesson Times

Don't switch lesson times unless you absolutely have to!

Many musicians, because of their busy performing schedule, feel the need to move their students' lesson times around. Try to do this as little as possible. You can easily double-book a student, or create confusion or frustration with a student that is constantly being shuffled around. The worst thing is double booking students and having to send them home. A student who is rescheduled too many times will quit. If a student's regular scheduled time no longer works for you, as the teacher, find a new regular time that does. I have worked with teachers who constantly call people (at the last minute, of course...), saying, "Hey, can you come in a half an hour early, so I can go home early tonight?" This is very unprofessional, and too common. Play this card as infrequently as possible, as you may need it for something more important than getting home early to watch TV.

Summertime Music Lessons

Many studios close in the summertime. I recommend you don't. If you feel entitled to enjoy the summer, feel free, but understand that at least fifty percent of your students who leave for the summer *won't* come back—no matter what they say, or what their intentions are. Even staying open, it is inevitable that you will lose students during the summer, and it is important to plan accordingly. *Plan on your income being down about 15 to 20 percent during the summer season.*

Another issue is students who stay during the summer but take extended vacations. I use this extra time between lessons to plan what I am going to do in the fall. Remember that the fall is a very big intake time for new students, and you can spend downtime during the summer in developing new marketing strategies, or improving your studio. I remind myself of this important process when I look out the window and see the sunshine.

Students often ask to change their lesson time during the summer. Suddenly, students who would normally come in at 4:30 P.M. want to come in at 10:30 A.M. I recommend not doing this unless it is convenient for you. Remember that the summer school break is only about two months, and most people can and will make do. You can very easily make your schedule insane by changing times for the summer only to change them *again* in the fall. This is, of course, before the sign-up for a new sport or activity! Try to keep things "business as usual" during the summer. We are a somewhat seasonal business, after all.

By doing a good job, you will make the decision difficult for a student who is considering taking the summer off. If your lessons are invaluable to your students, it becomes that much harder to leave! Also, what if you offered additional summer programs that created additional interest? This can help you create extra income and be a retention strategy at the same time.

CHAPTER 4 TAKEAWAYS

- Take time and plan for incoming phone calls and learn how to answer common questions.
- Create solid answers for difficult questions.
- Return calls promptly!
- Start lessons on time, end lessons on time.

CHAPTER 5

Observations and Suggestions for Teaching Guitar

"Creating relationships is vital to being successful in private lessons. It's so important to be engaged and to take a genuine interest in the student and what gets them excited. That's where you develop the bond. I really like to see things from the student's point of view and remain open minded. From there, it's so much easier to apply the knowledge and get the student involved. This is the real key to keeping students for the long haul. From there, they can really develop into the best musicians they can be."

—Jeff Moore, Guitar Teacher/Founder of
Interlude Music School
JeffAM.net

ORGANIZING THE LESSON

It is vital to learn how to pace your guitar lessons. Most teachers offer 30, 45, or 60 minute lessons, and the majority will tell you that a 30 minute lesson is the most challenging. Beginner teachers have difficulties pacing such a short lesson, as the time is over just when they get going.

As you start working with students, their personality and learning styles will begin to dictate your teaching methods. I always try to balance what the student wants with what the student needs.

If you are working on a song, it is very easy to create warm-up exercises, improvisation practice, and theory discussion around that one song. This gives the song more context and shows the application of these ideas, rather than just learning the techniques in isolation. I have found that this sticks with students.

There may be a technically difficult part of a song that can be unlocked by an exercise. I use this application for scales as well. If a song is based on the D Dorian mode, it's cool to show a student how to wrap that simple scale around a solo. Many guitarists get excited to learn a simple scale that will allow them to immediately start playing their own solos. Even though they do not have the vocabulary at this point, they can clearly hear how this works in the context of the music.

Some students will be scared to death by having to perform their own "solo." I set the bar really low here by offering just two or three notes on one string. I tell them that if they play these two or three notes, they can't possibly make a mistake. This always works.

Students often tell me that they hear music differently after they have been taking lessons for a while. This is great to hear because it means that their lessons are helping them develop their ears and a sense of musicality. To expand a student's listening skills is rewarding for the teacher as well.

It's a cue to make your lesson materials more succinct. Beginner students are the easiest to plan for, as they are starting at the very beginning. Despite this, some students learn the material very quickly, and others need extra time.

I keep a list of all of my teaching materials and put them in categories: theory, critical listening, warm-up exercises, scales, arpeggios, etc. I estimate how long each lesson takes to teach, so that if I have some extra time, I can segue into one of these other categories smoothly.

Always leave lesson time for questions. If you need to write notes for the students or record a segment of the lesson, leave time for that as well.

Don't make yourself late due to bad planning. I often put a breakdown of whatever the material is on mine or the student's phone, and then email that to them. Greg Arney (quoted in this book) uses Evernote to create a file for each student. I have known some teachers who put many of their most common examples on YouTube or Dropbox, and give the student access to save time.

Learn what gets each student excited about playing. Each student is unique, and the more you can accommodate different personalities and learning styles, the more successful you will be.

For returning students, take some time to engage them and listen to how they are doing and what is important in their life.

You can shuffle the content of your lessons as you see fit. I like to mix it up a little bit so that the student does not feel like things are predictable. In the winter, I might put more of an emphasis on warming up the fingers. Keeping students on a positive, upward trajectory is important.

Clearly explain the objectives of what you are teaching and what the desired results will be. Many students are intimidated about learning musical skills that you have possessed for years. Hopefully, you make it look effortless, but they might feel like it should come easy for them. I remind many beginner students that the first year I played guitar, it was difficult to master even the very basics. Always put yourself in the student's shoes.

For each new student, learn about their motivation for playing and what brought them to you. Explain how the guitar works. Demonstrate its sounds and how to properly hold it. Take the time to show how this alien object operates.

POSTURE AND HOLDING THE GUITAR

There are many ideas about how the guitar should be held, including a separate set of rules that apply to classical music. A common issue that I see repeatedly is the way the fretting hand is making contact with the strings. It is super important to get the students playing at the correct angle to get clearance to make notes and chords work. In my opinion, there are many ways to achieve this, as physical characteristics of the player will dictate this as well. Some guitarists, such as Steve Vai and Jimi Hendrix, possess long and thick fingers, which gives them technical opportunities that someone like B.B. King, with his short, thick fingers, would not have. It's important to recognize this and make it work for each student. Of course, as their fingers gain more strength, this will get easier. I remind them that getting the notes to ring clearly as opposed to being muted is usually a matter of 1/16 of an inch or less. It's much more vital to get the correct angle to create clearance. For students who struggle with this, spending time with the instrument is the best cure. Some beginner players can fret chords immediately, and some need a couple of weeks.

PRACTICE

Be detailed when you tell students how you want them to practice. Time? Repetitions? What has worked for you? Show the student how to practice. Practicing and just playing are not the same thing. Let them know that they can play all they like, but it's important to do the assignments you have given them. Estimate how much they will need to practice their assignments.

Patience

"Patience" is an overused word. There is a school of thought that great athletes, like Michael Jordan, can never be good coaches. Why? Because Michael Jordan could never understand why someone else can't do the things he can naturally and easily do. It's crucial to take a step back and understand that the majority of your students will have close to *no* musical experience. Many times, you have to convince them that they can learn how to play the guitar, but many *still* give up trying. There are also some people who just do not have much talent to work with. Interestingly, I find helping these students to play is very satisfying. This is something you can never forget or overlook.

TEACHER AS PSYCHOLOGIST

One key to being a good teacher is understanding the person in front of you. I don't treat all of my students the same way. Different concepts motivate people differently. If a student is attempting to enter a music college, there will be more pressure for them to meet goals to accomplish this. If the student is an adult "weekend warrior," you need to tread more lightly. Many musicians forget that the average player's goals and aspirations are very different from their own. To some, strumming a few simple tunes will accomplish their musical dream. Push the students that need to be pushed, but be careful not to try to force casual players into the guitar Olympics.

FASHION TIPS

Despite the stereotype of musicians as wild bohemians, I think it's important to look professional when doing your music lessons. You don't have to go "all corporate" and buy suits or other "business" attire. Do look "well put together," in whatever sense that means to you. It does make a difference as to how your business and service is perceived. Many students and parents of students are somewhat conservative. Accommodate them without feeling like a "sell out." Due to the nature of our business, we don't have the same dress code as attorneys (thankfully). It does not take much extra effort, money, or time, to look nice.

Remember, it's a big leap of faith for a parent to deliver their child to you, alone, in a practice room—some musician goon that they just met. Looking professional puts them at ease and gives you extra credibility.

LETTING STUDENTS PICK THEIR OWN MUSIC

When I first meet a student, I ask them what motivated them to pick up this instrument. I then have them pick a list of songs that they would (eventually) like to learn. This gets the students involved in what they play and learn. I tell them that if we can't learn the songs immediately, we can at least start developing the skills that will get them there. This is also a good way to get them out of a rut, since they can't blame you for forcing them to study some awful music that they didn't want to play. This can also be used as to advantage against our competition—the stereotypical teacher that has students go through a book without adding any extra value.

TAB VS. NOTATION

Many of the students you will be working with will simultaneously be "taking lessons" from YouTube. I don't necessarily see this as a bad thing, as it is often an indication that a student is involved beyond the lessons assignment. It's important to have many sources to learn from. That being said, too much emphasis on YouTube diminishes the importance of learning how to read and write music.

I will introduce simple reading basics (often just rhythmic ideas) to students to work in conjunction with other skills to be developed. This can work to "trick" them into getting to read if it is presented properly, and does not dominate the lesson, in the student's mind. As a student's interest in music and the guitar widens, it's important for you to teach them why reading and writing music is so valuable. Remind your students of these points:

- Music notation is truly an international language. Reading gives you the ability to communicate with any musician in the world. I often tell stories of my own world travels and how this is indeed the case.

- Not being able to read music is the musical equivalent of being illiterate.

But what about guitarists such as: Eric Clapton, Jimi Hendrix, Wes Montgomery, etc.? They didn't learn how to read music!!

Indeed, they did not. However, unless you are that one-in-a-zillion guy that can get to that level of playmanship, then you are limiting your opportunities in music by not learning how to read. I think it's great that many wind up playing in bands where reading is not required, but I do always encourage students to balance it out by learning notation.

The most valuable thing you can show a student is how to find their own voice and develop their own instincts. A guitar teacher can really be the guide that brings out the best in each student. I was once told that I ran my guitar group much like a football coach, and I took it as a compliment. It's critical to know when to push a student and when to lay off, and knowing what else is going on in their life is critical here. Understand their temperament: Are they competitive, and will they respond to challenges? Or do they need more support and caring words? This is some of the most valuable "teaching" you can do. Knowing a student's goals is important. They may never be more than a "rec" guitar player, so emphasize making learning fun, while getting your points across. Save your fire and brimstone for the student that says he wants to attend Berklee but doesn't do his homework!

DECODING MUSIC

One thing I find very useful for getting students to understand the mechanics of music is breaking down song forms in your lessons. Many of you will be dealing primarily with popular music. Once students are shown that many of the songs they want to learn are simply four chords, arranged in the different sections (verse-chorus-bridge, etc.), repeated for four or so minutes, then it becomes easier to take apart and learn.

Often, I will take a song and break it down into three or four smaller, more manageable sections. This prevents what I call "frontrunner's syndrome," which occurs when a student is only able to play the first part of a song well. It happens because the student practiced the first portion to death, while the rest of the song was left virtually unplayed. Neglecting the bridge is often a problem here, so I find that this method works really well.

One place I find this to be truly valuable is teaching students to read notation. Many students sound great on the first few measures, only to sound more discordant with every subsequent measure. Again, working with each system of half of a page, I break the song down into manageable sections. I use the 80/20 rule here: work on the 20 percent that is giving you 80 percent of the difficulty. People have a tendency to do it the other way around, so reinforcing this is important.

Some other things I have found that work for teaching notation or sight-reading:

- Before playing, just read through the piece. Look for anything that is problematic. What key is it in? Any key changes? Time signature changes?
- Before you play through the piece from the top, just play any passages that are the most difficult.
- If the student is playing the piece for the first time, start slowly.
- Play with a metronome. Sometimes students need to practice at a slower pace more than they need to learn a piece quickly.
- Check for "frontrunner's syndrome," and remind them to practice the piece evenly.

SWITCHING CHORDS AND OTHER BEGINNER GUITARIST'S NIGHTMARES

A big common denominator for beginner guitarists is the inability to switch chords in time. It's really important to let the student know that they are not alone in this, and that it is a problem for nearly everyone. I find, in general, that getting a new player over this hump can really get them into gear. Unfortunately, games like Guitar Hero have perpetuated the myth that playing a real guitar is just as easy as playing a video game. Not quite. Here are some techniques I use to address this problem:

1. Start off with two simple chords that are related by common tones or similar fingering. Example: in the first position: A minor to C, or C to F.
2. Have the student finger the chords without picking, just to get used to the muscle memory.
3. With the metronome set slow, have them play whole notes and switch the chords in time. This will give them plenty of time to switch, placing the emphasis on making the chord switch right on beat 1.

Once they have this, add more chords, increasing the metronome speed or start switching with half notes, quarter notes, eighth notes, etc.

This method is easy to scale across any chord progression, increasing in difficulty. It is a methodical and effective way to get through this barrier!

Barre Chords

Every beginner believes that he or she is the only person in the world who is challenged by barre chords, when in fact, everyone struggles with them. You will need lots of patience with some students who will struggle here. I will usually start by having students fret barre chords starting on about the seventh fret. This makes it easier to stretch and finger them. As the frets get wider apart, they can gradually move down to the lower frets, moving just one fret at a time. I often start with just a fifth string minor or minor seven barre chord, as I find this is the easiest to build from, and almost all of the other barre chords are a variation of this.

I have found that once students are able to get over this hump, it really opens up their playing. Many of them see that they are able to persevere and work through challenges that the guitar will bring.

Working with Rhythmically Challenged Students

If you remember your third grade music lessons, you remember that we are taught music is harmony, melody, and rhythm, presumably in equal parts. Rhythm is so important to make the music come alive. This can be difficult for some students, especially if they have no prior musical experience. How do we teach these difficult students?

If a student is just not getting it, I start by putting on some music. I will say, without giving any real instruction, "Tap your foot." Everyone can do this. It is intuitive. Of course, the beats may be rushed or behind, but it's a start. Once this is established, I tell the student that we are going to measure or add everything from this simple quarter note.

From here, I may ask to hear the beats out loud: 1, 2, 3, 4, etc. To keep it simple, I have them do this away from the guitar, to remove a level of confusion. Once the student can master this (within reason), we add the guitar, playing one open string in time. I will remind the student that if they are having difficulty rhythmically with a part, they can break this down to its lowest common denominator.

It is important that a student understand this progression. Of course, I recommend practicing with a metronome. A metronome is the single greatest way for a student to see improvement, as it's a measure of their ability. Giving a student specific take-home exercises (many of these are in my book *Absolute Beginner Guitar*) that address rhythm is another thing that I have found helpful.

In addition to this, I am a huge advocate of having students practice with the music they are trying to learn. This gets them "in the game" and helps sharpen many musical skills simultaneously. I often have students listen to the drums and the cues drummers provide as to where the song is headed. Playing with the music helps students improve at a rapid rate.

BUYING ADVICE FOR BEGINNER INSTRUMENTS

As a guitar teacher, you will often be asked to recommend instruments. This will happen with beginner students (many, who haven't taken a lesson) and with students looking to purchase their second or third guitar. Most of the emphasis here will be on beginners, but again, it will be helpful with any student ready to upgrade his or her guitar. Here are some questions to think about.

- *What is the age of the student?* The critical age for determining which guitar size to go with is about nine years old. Are they big enough to play a full sized guitar?

- *How tall is the student?* You don't want the student to be handicapped by an instrument that is way too big for them to play, so it's important to get the right fit. I have had beginner students that were dwarfed by their guitars. Luckily, they were able to return the instrument. If the guitar is just a little too big, they will grow into it in a short amount of time. Beginner guitars often keep their value as they are in high demand, and usually this will persuade parents to make the upgrade a year or so later to a full sized guitar. Keeping a ¾ guitar in your studio is not a bad idea. When students come in for a trial lesson you can fit them for the proper instrument.

- *Acoustic or electric?* You will often be asked to recommend whether a student should buy an acoustic or electric guitar. I always say to get the guitar that is closest to the type of music the student wants to play. There is a myth that the acoustic is easier and that simply is not the case; the electric guitar is physically easier to play. I've also heard people say that they want to start on the more difficult instrument, just because it is more difficult. This one I don't get at all. Help your students to choose the instrument they most want to play, and are the most comfortable actually playing.

- *Packs/bundles?* I recommend students buy guitar packs to get started. Guitar packs are good, one-stop shopping, in that they include all the accessories one needs to start playing. Generally, all guitar packs include a guitar, amp, tuner, picks, and strings.

Acoustic Guitars

- *Yamaha Gigmaker Standard:* This is a quality starter pack. They are generally about $150 new and are a great value. There is a "Deluxe" version of this that is about $50 more; it has a more ornate finish on the guitar, but plays the same. I think the Standard is a better deal.

- *Yamaha FG JR1 3/4 Size Acoustic Guitar:* This is another quality starter kit from Yamaha and is pretty much just the ¾ size of the Gigmaker.

Electric Guitars

- *Fender Squier.* I think Fender's "Squier" line is a very good beginner guitar. The quality is decent, and the Strat is a comfortable, versatile guitar. The trim levels of this seem to change often, so I will not recommend a specific one here. They generally run in the $175 to $200 range.

- *Fender Mini.* The Mini is the ¾ version of the Squier.

Intermediate Guitars

These days, there are several high quality, mid-level price range guitars. This market was much less competitive just a decade ago.

Some things to consider:

- What is the student's purpose for this guitar?
- Is it just the guitar they already have in a new color? I see this with Strats all the time! Suggest a guitar that they can keep for a while and one that will give them good value for their dollar.
- One common issue is students gravitating to a guitar that has a "Floyd Rose" style bridge. These can be tough to deal with if you are not aware of how to handle string changes and maintenance, so it's important to make students aware of this.

Generally, a student buying or having an interest in acquiring a new guitar is a good thing. It shows that he or she has taken a bigger interest in playing and is willing to invest time and money on exploring music in a much more serious way.

Where to Buy Guitars

In addition to local music stores, I often refer people to sites like Craigslist. This can be a good place to find guitars if the person is more price sensitive, or is willing to look for a great deal.

Affiliate Selling

Retailers like Guitar Center and Amazon are now offering Affiliate Selling Programs. This can be a great source of passive income, as it is possible to receive a percentage of sales without having to stock the instruments. In the case of Amazon, you can have a custom link on your website that directs the students to purchase instruments. You can add strings, picks, or whatever accessories you like. Eric Clemenzi (quoted in this book) sells instruments in his studio and offers select lines that are appropriate for his students. This is a great way to make students aware of brands that are lesser known but are great quality.

What About Amps?

Since all of the electric packs I recommend come with amps, this information might not apply to beginners who buy them.

Of course, every electric guitarist wants to march into Guitar Center and buy a 100 watt Marshall Stack, so it's important to guide the student. Does the student play in a band and need a bigger amp? Are they a "bedroom guitarist" that isn't likely to perform in public anytime soon? There are many options. The modeling type amps offer a ton of features and a large range in affordability. These amps have come a long way since they were introduced in the late nineties, and are exciting for many students as they offer a ton of features and neat sounds. If you are more of a purist, lower wattage tube amps offer real tube sound without having to carry around a huge amp, or worry about blowing out the windows of your house.

Last note: It is important here to get friendly with your local music store. If you bring sales to them, they will likely return the favor by referring students to you.

Assessing Beginner Students' Instruments

Many beginners have the misfortune of inheriting a guitar that has been in someone's basement for a long time. This disuse will usually handicap the player by leaving them with an instrument that has really high string action or buzzing frets or bridges. In many cases, a simple setup will fix this. Sometimes, the instrument will not be worth the investment of getting it repaired. Other times, just a few adjustments and some new strings will do the job. It's important to help the student make the call, here. Some of these instruments are of high quality, some are toys. Parents may be reluctant to spend money on a guitar repair; you can tell them that it will be better for the health of the guitar and more beneficial to the student to have this work done.

Do your students know how to change their strings? Show them! I have seen many hack string changes by beginners. Of course, the most common string to break is the high E, so I always tell students that sets are sold just for this string. Stock extras in your studio, as many lessons have come to a sudden halt because of a string break. I generally dedicate most of a half-hour lesson to string changing. I instruct them while changing the lower three strings and then have them change the top three while I watch.

A great tool to recommend is a guitar humidifier that can help regulate the wood flexing in acoustic guitars. This simple item pays for itself (about $15). If used regularly, your guitar will require less adjustments and maintenance.

DEALING WITH DIFFICULT STUDENTS AND PARENTS

There will always be challenges in dealing with the public. Without being unreasonable, sometimes it simply is not worth the money received for the effort and stress you will exert with certain students or their parents. A few years ago, I was about two hours away from having my entire schedule filled. I had three students that were problematic—not practicing, whiny parents, etc., and all three had lessons on the same day. And they all quit the same month! I immediately felt much more relaxed, and it didn't take long to replace them.

If someone is a problem, beyond not practicing their assignments, and you feel they are toxic to you and your business, do not hesitate to get rid of them. This sounds crazy to many people, but I assure you, it works. I don't want to burn bridges with people, but you literally can't please everyone. One student, I asked to leave because his mother called me all hours of the day and night, to discuss her son and pacify (even if temporarily) her neurosis. You are a music teacher and possibly an important person in a student's life. But you are not a servant. Having said this, I have only had to do this three times in the last ten years of teaching.

GETTING STUDENTS TO PRACTICE

Difficulty getting students to practice is a common problem. A key in this is finding what gets them excited about playing. One book that I like regarding this subject is *The Practice Revolution: Getting great results from the six days between lessons*, by Philip Johnston (Pearce, AU: PracticeSpot Press, 2004). Johnston makes the point that practicing is more effective in repetitions, not just in minutes. Despite this, you may have students who enjoy playing at the lesson, but have no inclination to practice outside of class. This can be justifiable with adults who pay for their own lessons, but younger students might have parents who are footing the bill and expecting tangible results. Work with them to help solve the problem.

Using sites like YouTube can work, but don't have it doing the lesson for you. Anyone can figure out that with YouTube as a constant companion, they eventually won't need you. I sometimes record small bits of the lesson on my iPhone and email it to the student to help with their assignment.

RETAINING STUDENTS

Here are a few strategies that go a long way in helping to retain students:

- Offer recitals (see page 78).
- Create group classes (ensembles) that get students more engaged. There is a huge social element to this as well.
- Be engaged while teaching. Don't "mail it in."
- Keep parents informed of progress (good or bad). Parents love encouragement and can be allies in helping to get the student on track.
- Expand what you do in your teaching: offer theory, listening, music history, or whatever your students seem to want.
- Offer a "Student of the Month" program. Reward students who are doing well. You can also reward them for milestone lessons: 25th guitar lesson, 50th guitar lesson, etc.
- Write a studio newsletter: Keep parents and students up to date with a newsletter. Companies like Constant Contact and Mail Chimp make this very easy and inexpensive to do. If you hate writing, trade services or pay a high school student to do it for you.

Remember, some students just won't catch on with your lessons. You can't please everybody. But take notice as to what makes a student a good fit or a bad fit. Building a relationship and being engaged with the student are the best ways to keep them interested.

SPORTS: THE ENEMY

I say this somewhat in jest, but it's vital to get to know the sport seasons in your area. Students also enroll in sports, and working around their sports schedule will be critical to keeping them enrolled in your studio. In the northeast, there are two primary times of year when sports start: September and April. Plan accordingly, and you should be okay. Obviously, if you are good at what you do, it will be harder for the student to give up your lessons for sports.

COMMON INJURIES

Yes, the guitar world can be a dangerous place. It's important that you make students aware of the injuries that can occur. The most common is tendinitis. I feel that many of these repetitive injuries can be avoided by using warm-ups (especially in the winter months). Encourage your students to do the same in their practice time. Make sure they are properly warmed up before trying difficult material. For many beginner players, there is a fine line between pushing them through the period where their hands are not strong enough from inexperience to overworking them. Make them aware that some pain is a normal part of starting guitar, especially when fingering barre chords.

Many teachers have had success using hand grippers that will help students safely build strength in their hands. This is a way to develop skill without the guitar necessarily being in your hands.

Other Student Injuries

Most of your students at some point will participate in sports activities. This will often lead to injuries. If a student is unable to play for a length of time, I will recommend that they keep taking the lessons while they are recovering. As a teacher, you can focus on teaching theory, doing critical listening, score analysis and breakdown, and many other topics. This can be a good thing, as it keeps the student engaged. The key with many students is scheduling and repetition, and if you are able to convince them of the value of this, you can keep them learning while they recover.

WHEN STUDENTS LEAVE

Students come, students go. Did you ever notice that events in life tend to happen in waves? You might have three new students call in one day, and then three students quit for totally unrelated reasons that you have no control over. Get used to it. It can be tough when this happens, but if someone decides to move, someone wants to take the summer off, or someone breaks their arm, there is nothing you can do about it. This is the natural flow of doing lessons.

When you lose students, try to get honest feedback on why they are leaving and learn from it. Always evaluate how you are doing your lessons and how you are running your studio. You can always improve your business and make it more efficient. It is a classic example of controlling what you can and not getting upset about what you can't.

CHAPTER 5 TAKEAWAYS
- Hone your craft, and learn from your mistakes.
- Have as much of the lesson environment planned in advance as possible.

CHAPTER 6

Getting to the Next Level

"I feel that the thirty minute lesson is so difficult at any age or any level, and I truly believe that students can benefit so much more by having the extra time. Parents need to see the progression and feel that once they can develop that love for music, it can benefit their child. Getting students' attention can be difficult, given all the activities they are involved with. I really emphasize hand position and will often take pictures for the student to reference where their hands should be on the guitar. This is something they can use when they practice and makes it easier for them to play effectively."

—Dan Searl, Guitar Teacher
DanSearl.com

Here are some things to think about as your studio expands:

BUILDING FROM WITHIN

One easy way to find new students is to market to people related to your current students. Siblings and parents are often inspired by the progress of a student and want to start playing themselves. This is a great way to "pick the low hanging fruit" while filling up lesson times. You can promote this sort of activity at peak times of the year.

Longer Lesson Times

Teachers often ask me for advice on how to book more students. One of the easiest ways to fill up your schedule is to look at your current roster. Many times, students who have been taking lessons for thirty minutes could be taking lessons for forty-five or sixty minutes. As a teacher, you will know if the interest level is there and whether the student is capable of handling a longer lesson time. There is, of course, a financial component here for the student as well. But if you have well qualified students who are interested, and who you like working with, increasing their lesson time can be an easy way to fill your schedule without having to spend extra money on marketing.

Referrals

Referrals are your number one way to get good, qualified students through your front door. How do you generate referrals? Try different approaches, to see what works best for you. Many studios have "bring a friend week" or give a free lesson, for referrals. These are good ideas. I always send a gift to any student that has referred someone to us. I am also willing to give a free or discounted lesson to someone that is a referral, though this is not usually necessary. Often, by the time a referral calls to book a lesson, they have already made up their mind, and it's an easy sell.

Repairs

Are you the handy type? If so, have you considered learning to do some simple guitar repairs? This can be an easy way to make some extra money. The majority of the work is simple setups and occasionally some pickup installs. These repairs don't require a ton of specialized tools. If you aren't handy, perhaps you can partner with a local repairman who is.

Selling Accessories

Our studio sells accessories, like strings, picks, and instructional books. We carry these items mainly for convenience, and we don't receive a lot of revenue from them, but that doesn't mean that you won't. Establishing a resale relationship with a company can be surprisingly easy and will allow you to buy items at dealer or wholesale prices. You will need an Employer Identification Number (EIN), which you can receive in minutes after filling out the online application at IRS.gov, and a commercial location. If there are other services you can offer such as repairs, let people know about them. Not only is it a convenience to your students, but it can be another great source of revenue. Eric Clemenzi (quoted in this book) has had success selling instruments at his studio.

I have also become a reseller of Hal Leonard Corp.'s products. They offer special deals for teachers and have thousands of books and DVDs that are great additions to your teaching library.

Don't forget the sales tax....

Many teachers who do sell their own accessories need to be aware of sales tax. Reporting and filing sales tax is easy, but it is often found in a tax audit as unrecorded income. Keep track of what you sell. These numbers will also help you to keep track of what's hot and what's not in your inventory. Programs like QuickBooks can help you with this.

Selling Gift Certificates

Throughout the year and specifically during the holidays, we sell a lot of gift certificates. This is a great opportunity to have your lessons be a great gift, and it definitely helps increase your name recognition, as well. North Main Music uses a custom designed gift certificate, but you can use a stock one if you like. People will usually buy a set amount of lessons and call back once they are ready to book a lesson time.

Here are a couple of odd things I have noticed about gift certificate students and sales.

- *More than **half** of them are never used.* This sort of makes sense, because it was someone else's idea for the lessons and not the actual receiver's, whether they wanted lessons or not.

- Less than 50 percent of the students continue taking lessons after the gift certificate is used. This can be for many reasons but again, since it wasn't their idea, their long-term commitment to you is less.

FIG. 6.1. North Main Music Gift Certificate

One effective use of gift certificates is offering them to charities. I will phone non-profit organizations in our area and offer to donate gift certificates to any raffles they may be having in the near future. This is great for the charity, and it gets our name out there often with free advertising. Donating lessons drives potential new students in your front door and gives you a tax write off (you will need as many as you can get) for delivering the lessons. Did I mention it's a nice thing to do for your community?

Recitals

Once you have good, working relationships with your students, and are pleased with the results, having a *recital* is a tremendous way to celebrate their progress. A recital works on many levels:

- Students who participate in recitals are much more likely to be long-term students.
- Recitals are a great way to get students motivated and have them work toward an event.

- Parents love recitals, as it gives them a chance to see how their child is progressing and where their money is (wisely) being spent.

- Recitals are a great way to help students experience the joy of performing or overcoming the fear of performing.

We have been running recitals for years, now, and I thoroughly enjoy seeing students improve from recital to recital. It really is a testament to the dedication and enthusiasm that teachers give to their students. It does not go unappreciated.

A few notes about running recitals....

Many teachers are apprehensive about charging money for tickets. If the show is costing you money, charge. I have had one person complain about being charged for the recital, among the thousands of tickets we have sold. Provided the show is good, most people are not concerned with the face value of the recital ticket. They are totally focused on seeing their loved ones play,

Look for venues in your area that can work with you to put on the show. If you are lacking a PA system and a space to host the event, try offering to host your show on an off time at another venue, perhaps a Saturday or Sunday morning.

We work with a local music venue that is great and provides the backline for the show. This is a win-win deal, as the venue gets proceeds from the show, and the ease of setup and location of the venue is good for us. Local libraries, churches, and schools can sometimes host recitals, as well.

Raising Tuition

Okay, so now you are doing well. You have some students and are starting to see a little financial success. Eventually, you will have to raise tuition, because let's face it, the prices of all services and products go up. Especially in times of recession, teachers are reluctant to raise their rates, but it's important not to think this way. We are not talking about raising your fees dramatically. Do something that makes sense, in the 5 to 10 percent range. If you charge $25 per lesson, moving up to $27 can be a relatively small amount for an individual student, but across all your students over a year, it can significantly add to your profitability. A good time to do this is in September when you generally start to enroll new students. Make sure you do not come across as reactive or defensive. Most clients will respond with "A buck or two a lesson isn't a big deal." Your students have already committed to you and your studio. A small increase will not sink you, but it may push some people out who were looking to quit anyway.

Helping Kids Get into College

The most simultaneously challenging and rewarding students for me are students that are planning to study music in college. If these students are home grown (they started playing with you), it is clear that you have made an impact in helping them to progress and to see their musicality as a real career opportunity. The biggest thing that I think you need to make clear to students looking to attend a music college is the amount of work that it will take to get and stay there, and how stiff the competition is. It is one thing to be a hot-shot player in your hometown, but quite another when you enter most good music schools.

A common question I will ask a student is, "Can you see yourself working on music for twelve hours a day, at least five days a week?" If their answer is "No," or "I don't know," I tell the student he or she needs to reevaluate. Another common misconception is that music students in college do nothing but jam all day. Music programs all have a certain amount of core classes in general education that have to be fulfilled.

Of course, your personal experiences here are invaluable to prospective college students. One important thing I learned from attending Berklee is that some classes were more interesting to me than others. Forcing myself to push through the more arduous classes made me realize that in this sense, every job and every school is a similar situation. There are always assignments, projects, or events that we are required to complete, and our ability to finish them without being selective can serve us well in any situation.

To illustrate this point, I will ask students, "Who would you like to trade jobs with in the industry?" Let's say the answer is John Mayer. I promise them that despite his success, John has many obligations to his career that aren't always the most pleasant or entertaining. I think it's important that students understand this.

Have a very specific plan of how you are going to prepare each student. If the student is a junior, encourage them to visit the campus and spend some time learning about the programs. Urge them to watch student performances. This alone can fire them up and send them back to the woodshed. Despite warning them about the competitive nature of college music programs, they need to see it with their own eyes. If students are targeting specific colleges, see if the school runs any type of summer programs. This will allow students to become friendly with instructors and to see firsthand how things operate. Attending these summer programs can help the student and the college figure out whether they are a good match for one another.

Encourage students to take private lessons with someone from the school's faculty. This would, of course, be in addition to private lessons with you! Paying extra for these lessons is a relatively small investment for a large return, as this teacher could help the student by telling them exactly what it will take to study at that school. With Skype, this is possible just about anywhere. The student may also be able to use this teacher as a reference when applying at the college.

In your own lessons, really work towards improving whatever the student's weaknesses are. In many cases, the weakness is music reading (sad but true). At this level, it is imperative that the student understands that not being able to read music well is going to make it a rough ride in any college music program. If students are not currently participating in their school music program, you should strongly encourage them to do so. I have found that high school programs are a great way to improve reading skills, simply by the amount of time that they are exposed to it. You can't possibly give them that exposure in a weekly hour or half hour lesson. The interest in studying music at the collegiate level is often the tonic to get kids more committed to reading, as they know it will be imperative to succeeding.

Discuss what majors your students are thinking about studying. Ask them what their career ambitions are, and then try to direct them to people or resources you have access to. Many high school musicians have strange and delusional ideas about how this industry works, and many parents, who are far removed from the industry, have even weirder ideas. Erroneously, it is a popular belief that careers in music are feast or famine only; you are either Jimi Hendrix or you are out of work. There are many jobs in between that can give you a career.

If possible, help your students with any demo materials that need to be submitted, as well as preparing them for any auditions.

Auditions

Once the student has decided on some schools that they would like to attend, the next step is to find out what each school requires for entry. Some schools require audition pieces that are chosen by the player in a particular style, while others prefer having the students play a pre-arranged piece. Challenge the student to learn the pieces inside and out! The best cure for nerves on an audition is preparation. Cover all areas of the upcoming audition. If a student is weak in improvisation, spend the most time on this. We all have a tendency to work on the things that we are already good at.

If you have a student that is participating in a school music program, encourage them to try out for All State. This is a great résumé builder, and if the student qualifies, will give them an opportunity to play with other talents who made All State. This type of experience can help them tremendously.

Here are some general tips I have given students for auditions:

- *Dress well.* Yes, it matters! Show that you care about the audition and are serious about doing well.

- *Spend some time thinking about questions you may be asked.* Always respond with assertive answers. What do I mean by this? Teenagers have a bad habit of answering everything with "I don't know" and "maybe." These are what I call lazy words, so don't use them. Adults genuinely love talking to young people that have a clear sense of themselves and who they are.

- *Thank whoever is doing the audition for taking the time to meet with you.* No matter how grumpy they are!
- *Listen more than talk.* Remember the old joke; you have never said anything you didn't already know.
- *Make eye contact.* This is another positive way to engage.

Similar rules apply to any in-person scholarship auditions. Encourage your students to look around for them as there are many out there.

Even if students are not potential elite players, can you see them being able to survive and thrive in a college situation? Sometimes other skills (production, business, etc.) are real talents the student should accentuate in a college situation.

BUILDING FROM THE OUTSIDE

Using Local Colleges

Check local colleges in your area to see if they are offering any type of music program. Many of them offer *nothing*. This can be an opportunity to try to start one or at least offer one for non-credit. This will take some persistence on your part, as most schools are difficult to motivate into unknown territory. The advantage you will have is that it will cost the school close to nothing to offer this sort of program, as all they will really need to do is find some unused space. This is exactly how I started teaching at Rivier University. I understood that the school was going to offer my class and do little else in terms of promoting it. So, I promoted the class on campus with my own flyers and public performances. Word of mouth—those referrals we talked about earlier—also helped me build my program tremendously. Expect to be persistent contacting administration. I recommend speaking on the phone, as email is easy to ignore and delete.

Get involved in local events. Music is featured just about everywhere. This is a tremendous opportunity for people to learn about what you do. Playing for senior centers, local Chambers of Commerce, Lions or Rotary groups, and local cafés and bookstores can help to raise your profile.

What about Public Schools?

You can attempt to do similar after-school type programs at your public schools, or at the very least, befriend local music teachers, in hopes of offering guitar lessons there. But I have had surprisingly less success here. Here is my theory:

As school programs continue to be cut every year and teachers worry about whether they will have a job next semester, I believe public school teachers are increasingly reluctant to work with outside teachers (you) as they don't want to threaten their position or "rock the boat" with administration. I have verified this with many public school teachers privately. Despite my misgivings, I think having teachers advocate for you as a private music teacher, or giving you opportunity to offer additional programs, is worth the effort.

I do currently run an after school program. This has been very successful, but was turned down by several schools until one principal strongly advocated it. This is a classic example of the more times you swing the bat, the more you will hit something. If you have a relationship with a music teacher, find a way that you can help them.

Newspaper Ads

Running newspaper ads is a dying art form. Be careful not to place too much stock ($) into newspaper ads, as newspapers are quickly going the way of the dinosaurs. With that in mind, there *may* be some good print advertising opportunities, depending on your market. One thing I have had success with is advertising on the front of newspapers with a "stick it" note. These tend to work better in small, focused markets. A much better way to get in the paper is by doing what you do really well: public performances, recitals, etc.

Partner with Other Businesses

Many businesses in other industries are competing for the same geographic (clients) and will usually be very interested in sharing advertising opportunities. At the very least, you might strike a deal to advertise your lessons in their business in exchange for the same in yours. I can't even count how many students in our studio take either dance classes or martial arts. Finding teachers who offer lessons for instruments that you don't teach can be a great way to align with other studios. You could possibly partner together on recitals or other public events.

Brand Advertising

One thing to think about when advertising is how long the advertising piece will stay around. Does it run in the Sunday paper or does it sit around on a calendar for a month? Is it the type of advertising that encourages people to buy now, or is it "image" type advertising that reinforces a brand? I find the best advertising is the type that makes you call now or within a short time span. For my studio, the best times to run ads are in September when school gets back in session, and right after the holidays when people frequently get new instruments. The rule of thumb is to advertise when you expect the most interest. Ice cream stands offer sales during the dog days of summer because summer is the peak season for ice cream.

What Type of Advertising Do *You* Like?

Any easy way to answer this is to think about what you respond to. Study ads from all industries and see what you can use. Many people just stay in their own field of interest, but I have learned many things from ads in other industries. McDonalds or Starbucks have great ideas you can learn from.

Payback of Advertising

When placing an ad, think about what the payback will be. How much is a student worth? Sometimes, you can figure a student can be worth, say, $500 to $600. You can calculate this by taking current students and adding up how long they have been taking lessons from you. This can help you make an informed decision when spending money on advertising. *If* you can keep a student you obtained from an advertisement for a long period of time, then it was a good investment.

Offering Online Lessons

Online lessons can be a great way to expand your business. By using Skype, FaceTime, or Google Chat, you can grab a worldwide market that can attract extra students. Depending on where the students are from, online lessons can be an effective way to fill down times because of the difference in time zones.

YouTube and the Free Society

Now, and in the future, it will be important to prove the value of what you are offering. Many people who are under 25 have never paid for a book (Kindle books are too easy to steal), never paid for music (that war was lost in 2001 by Napster), and seldom pay to go to the movies (streaming is widely available).

I have experienced this with what I call "YouTube" guitarists. These are people who have taken a variety of free online lessons that, while useful, have created giant gaps in their playing. It is important to position yourself as someone who is worth the extra money: not only to fill in the gaps, but to provide a one-on-one teaching experience that is much more valuable than learning from a canned one-way online video. This, I believe, will be the biggest challenge of guitar teachers in the present and future.

You Are in Competition with Everyone Else

As guitar teachers, we tend to think our competition is only other guitar teachers. Remember that you are in competition with every other leisure activity out there. At the end of the day, people only have so much time and money to devote to extracurricular actives. What are other activities that people (in particular, kids) participate in? Marital arts, sports, school clubs, and tutoring are just a few examples. That being said, it's not a bad idea to study these competitors to see if you can learn anything valuable as you are competing for the same audience.

CHAPTER 6 TAKEAWAYS

- Find easy ways to grow your business from your existing student base.
- Carefully look for new ways to attract students.
- Find other businesses in your community that you can work together with.

CHAPTER 7

Deeper Inside the Business

"It's so important to listen to your students and keep them excited. What's worked for me as a teacher is learning how to take a student's 'no,' and move through it. Sometimes, it's important to have students work outside of their comfort zone and do things they aren't familiar with. This keeps it fresh and challenging. I find it very easy to stay motivated as a teacher, and I learn from every student that I work with."

—Jason Latham

The process of running and perfecting your business never stops. You should always be looking for new ways to grow your studio, for new ideas and new ways to make it run more smoothly. Don't neglect this end of it. Many studio owners get started with students, do well, and then do *nothing* to maintain or grow their business. Always remember that your business is a living, breathing organization, and that nothing in our world stays the same. Everything either grows or dies. Stay current, and always look for ways to remain relevant.

BUDGETING YOUR TIME

When you are working on your business, it's very important to avoid getting caught up in day-to-day minutia. Think of what action will accomplish the most and will have the biggest impact on your business, and then prioritize what you are doing. When making a list for the week, the month, or the year, I ask myself what will have the biggest impact and what are the most important to do? Then I think about the order the actions need to be completed. Many people will worry about small, less critical items that can often be done later. If your focus is getting more clients, then your most important action item is to figure out how to get more clients. Stick to the larger tasks and methodically go through them. The book *The 4-Hour Workweek* (Expanded and Updated Edition) by Timothy Ferriss (New York: Harmony Books, 2009) has some great ideas on this subject. I highly recommend you read it.

BUSINESS INSURANCE AND WHY YOU NEED IT

To work in a home office or commercial space, you will have to acquire business insurance for your company's property, the people who come into that property (students, parents, and employees), and the possibility of having to temporarily shut down business due to a natural disaster. Why do you need this? Simply, because the cost of someone getting injured or suing you could bankrupt your personal and business finances.

When seeking insurance quotes, make sure you ask about business property insurance to protect all of your workplace property. This type of insurance is very similar to homeowner's insurance and protects both your property and your business equipment in case of a natural disaster or other accident. That same natural disaster might also cause a temporary interruption in your work, which would require a separate insurance policy, known as "business interruption insurance." This policy covers financial losses that you may experience at that time; it may be part of your normal business policy.

Furthermore, you need to have coverage for your own liability. A *general liability* insurance policy protects you in case someone other than yourself or your employees is injured while on your business property.

A *business owner's policy*, also known as a *BOP*, combines several of these policies into one. When getting a business owner's policy, make sure you understand what is and isn't covered, and what additional insurance coverage you may need. A landlord usually demands that you carry this type of policy. They are surprisingly inexpensive: about $30 per month for a million dollar policy, where my business is. It's important to note that you will need business insurance if you do lessons at schools, churches, etc.

PAYING TAXES

Once you start working for yourself, your tax status changes. Usually as someone else's employee, you will pay taxes by the year. Being self-employed, you must pay taxes every quarter. If you are saving money for taxes, you will have no problem paying quarterly taxes. Personally, I like to pay my federal taxes monthly so that it is a recurring expense I have budgeted for and not something that I am saving for. Many people like to hold their money and wait until the last possible minute to pay. Either way is fine, but don't get blindsided by the amount you owe for taxes. This is just a reality of running your own business. You also may be responsible for state taxes. The details differ state by state, so check with your state's guidelines. If you haven't already, this may be a good time to think about forming an LLC or similar corporate structure.

It is beyond the scope of this book to offer in-depth tax advice. I will say that many musicians I talk to have found that getting half-assed advice from their dad, or someone who knows just enough to be dangerous, is usually *not* a good idea. Seek the professional advice of someone who can help you and who can understand your situation. Financial advice is a service that *more* than pays for itself and will save you money. In the long run, it is not a wise decision to be cheap finding a good tax consultant. Do research on accountants, and request a fifteen-minute free consultation to see if they have a good feel for the type of business that you are running. A knowledgeable tax consultant can save you a lot of money in the long run, and can prevent you from making many financial mistakes.

Here is my simplification on taxes and how they work:

When you earn money for a lesson, about 30 percent goes to federal taxes. Having fun yet? If it makes you feel any worse, about 53 cents of every dollar you earn will go to some sort of tax, be it car registration, property taxes, and so on, and so on, and so on. If you plan on putting money aside for Uncle Sam, 30 percent is a good number to start with.

The biggest mistake I see people make with their taxes is that they put *nothing* aside and hope they get lucky at tax time. This is foolish, and will probably cost them lots of money that they probably have not saved. A few business owners fail to report income to the IRS and wait to see how long they can get away with it. As cash is becoming an endangered species in our credit/debit card–based banking system, not reporting income has become much more difficult to get away with. A few minutes into a tax audit is all the IRS needs to figure it out.

Some good news: As a business owner, you do have tremendous advantages in countering this system. First off, any expenses incurred for business are tax write-offs. This makes your taxable income lower. Examples of things that you can use for write offs:

- *Internet Service*
- *Leased Space.* If you are teaching at home, you *may* be able to get a home office deduction, if that space is used exclusively for business. The utilities for this location, as well as any other operating expenses, would be included. Keep in mind, this is only for the space used for business and not common areas.
- *Mileage.* Report only the mileage on your car used for business reasons. Examples: That trip to the copy store, or the day you put flyers up all over town.
- *Phone.* Since your phone is used for business, it is now possible to write off some, or possibly all of it.
- *Ads/Flyers*
- *Professional Services.* Accountants, attorneys, etc.
- *Lessons.* Do *you* still take lessons? You can write those off, too.
- *Instruments or equipment purchased for business.* You will be able to write these off, as well.
- *Business Seminars/Music Seminars.* Continuing education costs.
- *Traveling/Entertainment Expenses.* That applies to travel-ling, eating, and entertaining for business purposes.

- *Gear.* Any equipment that you use in your business purchased before its actual formation can be sold at a later date to the business and taken as a deduction. And who thought all that money you wasted due to Gear Acquisition Syndrome wouldn't be of some use? Keep in mind that the gear then belongs to the business, not to you, and having insurance is key. Without insurance, you could lose your instruments, if you are sued. With this in mind, you may want to keep some instruments out of the business (vintage guitars?).

The Write-Off Myth

I sometimes hear people boast, "I can just write it off!" Just because there are many instances where you may indeed write off purchases, restaurants, and entertainment, that doesn't mean that everything you do is free. Deductions will give you a discount against your taxes, but remember, it has to be for your business, and you can count on the amount you get back usually being about 30 percent or less. This is an over simplification, but it will give you a good, round number to use when estimating your expenses.

Taxes are a loaded topic, and I highly recommend doing more reading on the subject and consulting with a tax professional. Many people have a shocking number of half-truths they use to prepare their taxes and try to write off some silly things. So no, you can't write off the new backyard pool!

BUDGETING YOUR MONEY: YOU DON'T NEED EVERYTHING NOW!

I have seen other studios with really great equipment, programs, or locations, and have impatiently wanted to have everything they have...NOW! This feeling is not uncommon; it's very natural. But I understand that budgeting a certain amount of money each month to improve or repair my facilities is a great way to keep from becoming overwhelmed financially by too many expenses. Start off with what will have the most benefit and will stretch your money the furthest. Replace light fixtures, have your instruments tuned or repaired, and buy nicer fixtures or artwork. In the beginning, you may be forced to simply use what you already own. Make a plan for what you want to eliminate or upgrade. I have had good luck with Craigslist and used office supply stores. Many times, you can get significant discounts for gently used items. Remember, reinvesting in your studio is also a tax benefit.

A few first-time teachers have come to my school and asked me, "How can I do all of this, are you kidding?" I tell them to keep in mind that developing these programs and getting their school where they want it can take years, and it is never a finished project. Like any other skill that you are trying to perfect, it takes practice and patience. With this in mind, it is important to set goals and to think about where you want your studio to be three months from now, six months from now, and one year from now. Ask yourself what it is going to take to meet those goals. This will make it easier for you to move forward at your own pace. After a few months, you will see a difference in your studio.

FINANCING WITH CREDIT CARDS

You might not have the cash on hand to get your studio up and running, as you would like. While I am not a big fan of financing shopping sprees with credit cards, these days, many small businesses are started and sustained on credit cards.

If you are doing any type of advertising, you may be able to get a deal where you can pay in monthly installments to alleviate the pain of spending your hard-earned cash all at once. Even if you can pay at once, it might be a better deal if the creditor is willing to stretch out the payments for three or six months. An important thing to note here is the difference between buying unnecessary items and leveraging. If, for example, it is necessary to finance something that costs $5,000 but can make your business much more viable, then this type of debt can be somewhat justified. Just be careful with the justification!

HSA ACCOUNTS AND PROVIDING YOUR OWN HEALTH INSURANCE

Pop Quiz: What is the number one cause of bankruptcy among individuals in the United States? Did you guess medical bills? You guessed right! As nice as your doctors are, a trip or two to see them can be very expensive, and good luck if you really get sick or hurt. Many young people who are not covered by their parents' insurance and choose to remain uninsured are playing a dangerous game. Medical bills can get into five digits before you blink and can set you back for years. It's important to get some information on how to get insured and perhaps even find a tax benefit.

It is way beyond the scope of this book to thoroughly cover the multitude of insurance options available, as they differ from state to state. One option I like is the health savings account (HSA). This is potentially a great option for many self-employed professionals (SEPs), such as musicians.

Here is how it works:

An HSA is a tax-advantaged medical savings account available to taxpayers in the United States who are enrolled in a high-deductible health plan. Funds contributed to an account are not subject to federal income tax at the time of deposit. The funds roll over and accumulate year to year, if they are not spent. HSA funds may be used to pay for qualified medical expenses at any time without federal taxes liability or penalties.

Supporters of HSAs believe that they help reduce the growth of health care costs and increase the efficiency of the health care system. HSAs encourage saving for future health care expenses and allow patients to receive needed care without a gatekeeper to determine what benefits are allowed. HSAs make consumers more responsible for their own health care choices through the required High-Deductible Health Plan (HDHP.)

The premiums for an HSA are less than the premiums for traditional health insurance. A higher deductible lowers the premium rate because the insurance company no longer pays for routine healthcare. Insurance underwriters feel people who see a relationship between medical cost and their bank accounts will require less medical care and shop for lower-cost options.

In catastrophic situations, an HSA participant's maximum out-of-pocket expense can be less than that of a person participating in a traditional health plan. This is because a qualified HDHP can cover 100 percent after the deductible, and doesn't involve coinsurance.

HSAs also give you some flexibility not available in most traditional health plans; you can use your HSA to pay for qualified medical expenses not covered in standard or HSA insurance plans on a pretax basis. This could include dental, orthodontics, vision, and other approved expenses. Over time, if medical expenses are low and contributions are made regularly to the HSA, the account can accumulate significant assets. These assets can be used for health care tax free, or used for retirement on a tax-deferred basis.

In closing, an HSA gives you an opportunity to direct your own health spending and get a pretax write-off. Deductibles are often high ($5,000 and up) but accumulated over a few years, this can add up to big savings. The key here is to have some sort of coverage.

CHAPTER 7 TAKEAWAYS

- Now that you have some students, solidify your lessons business by making it internally stronger.

- Get on your taxes before they get on you.

- Plan on getting insurance; you'll need it.

CHAPTER 8

Moving on Up: Commercial Space Considerations

"Communicating with all types of people really helps, whether they are musicians or not. Don't be shy or embarrassed about your talent; having that authority as a teacher is the key. When you are doing lessons, listen to what the students feel like they need. Being a facilitator, not a dictator, will empower them to make choices. It is tough to tell students that they won't necessarily sound like the musician they want to in a short period of time. Developing a good sound can take a long time, and students need to stick with it."

—Nanette Perrotte, Music Teacher
nanettelux.blogspot.com

LEASING A COMMERCIAL SPACE

I have already talked about the upside of having commercial space. If you have made the commitment to take your business out of your house and into a commercial space, there are many concepts you will need to think about.

The Space Itself: The Lease

You are at a distinct disadvantage if you have not negotiated a commercial lease before. In the commercial world of real estate, there are many rules that favor the lessor (the landlord/owner) and not the lessee (you), which can often mean that you are betting against the house. The main points that will be negotiated are:

- *Price:* Rents in the Northeast are often calculated by price per square foot. Simply put, if the property is 1,000 square feet and the per-square foot price is $10 (PSF), the price per month is $10,000.

- *Term:* What is the length of the lease? It is usually to your advantage to have a shorter termed lease. Two to three years is usually fair. If your business is new, you may want to push for a two-year lease. Landlords are usually willing to invest more in the deal for fit-ups, if you are staying for a longer term.

- *Security deposit:* You will usually need a decent amount of money to get into a space. Count on first month's rent, security deposit (usually the equivalent of one month's rent), and (usually) the last month's rent to be paid up front. I would not try to negotiate on these points, as it gives the perception that you have no money and is not a good sign for a long, fruitful relationship, from the landlord's perspective.

- *Option to renew:* Some leases require you to commit to renew, or not renew, the lease within (say) sixty days before it expires. Though this clause is not usually enforced, you should decide whether you will stay in the space well before your lease is up. Many people feel the pressure to renew their lease, as they are afraid they will lose the space. Believe me, if you are a good tenant, you are in a good position here. Under normal circumstances, no landlord (unless he has rocks in his head) would want to lose you. Many people become "tenants at will" and have a lease that is a month-to-month. If you feel this is good for you (you may be looking for a new space), then consider this option.

- *Maintenance:* Who pays for repairs to the unit? Count on issues with the HVAC (heating/ventilating/air conditioning) of the space you are renting during the life of the lease. This can cost big bucks if the onus is on you. Perhaps you will only be responsible for changing filters, or doing checkups on the unit, or maybe all of it will be covered by the landlord. Whatever the case, read carefully. You may want to pay to have the unit inspected ($100 or so) by an independent contractor even if your landlord tells you it's okay.

- *Utilities:* Are the utilities included? It's amazing how we all pay more attention to the bill when we are paying for it. One important issue is to see whether there is a separate gas bill. Is it covered? I once had a unit I agreed to pay the utilities (electric) for and then received a separate gas bill. Problem was, the gas was being split on the meter with my neighbor, who had this included in his rent. Needless to say, in his unit the AC was never off in the summer and the heat was never off in the winter. The landlord split it according to the percentage of used space and billed me the percentage. Do you think I was getting a fair shake? Remember that paying for utilities may get you leverage somewhere else.

- *Fit-up costs:* What condition is the carpet in? Do the walls need paint? An HVAC system? If the carpets are trashed and someone painted the place pink, don't let the landlord act like they are doing you a favor by replacing and repainting. These are just common re-fit expenses that the landlord will incur, regardless of what kind of tenant rents the space. What if you need something modified? Then, you and your landlord may work out a deal to add time to the lease, or pay out of pocket, to have a wall put up or bathroom put in, etc.

- *How long has the space been empty?* Do some digging. Look online and see if you can get additional info on the property. The longer it has been empty, the better your bargaining position. Talk to other tenants and see how the property is handled. How long have they been there? How is their relationship with the landlord?

- *Comparable rents:* Look for other similar spaces in your area. Is your place a bargain? Why is one area of town more expensive than another?

- *What is the allowed usage of the space?* You may want to have your lease stipulate that the space is to be used for music lessons and add a description of what instruments are used. Many landlords will not be thrilled about the prospect of music lessons in their space, and it's important that you do not disturb the other tenants. One thing that helps is that most lessons take place later in the day and many "professionals" finish around 5:00 P.M.

- *Will leasing the space add any value to your lessons?* Is it an upgrade from where you are teaching now?

Nets

In commercial real estate, a *net lease* requires the tenant to pay, in addition to rent, some or all of the property expenses that normally would be paid by the property owner (known as the "landlord" or "lessor"). These include expenses such as real estate taxes, insurance, maintenance, repairs, utilities, and other items.

The items that are to be paid by the tenant are usually specified in a written lease. For properties that are leased by more than one tenant, like a shopping center, the expenses that are "passed through" to the tenants are usually prorated among the tenants based on the size (square footage) of the area occupied by each tenant. The term *net lease* is distinguished from the term *gross lease*. In a *net lease*, the property owner receives the rent "net" after the expenses that are to be passed through to tenants are paid. In a *gross lease*, the tenant pays a gross amount of rent, which the landlord can use to pay expenses or in any other way as the landlord sees fit.

This is something that can get out of hand quickly. These types of leases give the landlord tons of flexibility as his rising costs of taxes and maintenance can get passed on to you. Landlords often juice the numbers when it comes to building upkeep to steadily raise your rent. It is important to get a handle on how this works.

There are standard names in the commercial real estate industry for different sets of costs passed on to the tenant in a net lease.

- *Single net lease:* In a single net lease (sometimes shortened to Net or N), the lessee or tenant is responsible for paying property taxes as well as the base rent. Double- and triple-net leases are more common forms of net leases because all or the majority of the expenses are passed on to the tenant.

- *Double net lease:* In a double net lease (Net-Net or NN), the lessee or tenant is responsible for property tax and building insurance. The lessor or landlord is responsible for any expenses incurred for structural repairs and common area maintenance. "Roof and structure" is sometimes calculated as a reserve, a common amount is equal to $0.15 per square foot.

- *Triple net lease:* A triple net lease (Net-Net-Net or NNN) is a lease agreement on a property where the tenant or lessee agrees to pay all real estate taxes, building insurance, and maintenance (the three "nets") on the property in addition to any normal fees that are expected under the agreement (rent, premises utilities, etc.). In such a lease, the tenant or lessee is responsible for all costs associated with the repair and maintenance of any common area.

  This form of lease is most frequently used for commercial freestanding buildings. However, it has also been used in single-family residential rental real estate properties. The landlord asking for triple net has become a lot more common. The good news is that you will likely only need a small amount of space to rent (250 to 500 square feet perhaps), so you are a little less likely to encounter this.

Variations on this are called "modified gross leases" and "full gross leases" among others. This is a big one, so do your homework! Check the suggested books section at the end of this book!

Strategies for Negotiation

Here are a few suggestions for negotiating your lease.

Understand what is important to the landlord when going into a lease. His concern is having a fully leased building with rents as high as the market will bear. This improves the resale of the building and also gives him additional leverage with a bank if he chooses to refinance. You might be tempted to negotiate the price per square foot and negate everything else, but you can find other, equally effective ways to lower your actual costs. This situation is very similar to buying a car. You think you got a great, low sale price on the car—only to find out that your interest rate on the car loan is sky high.

Start off the negotiation about 20 to 25 percent lower than the price you expect to pay. Calculate the value of the following:

- *Fit up*
- *Utilities*
- *Does the rent increase during the duration of the lease?* Many landlords will ask for an increase of 3 to 5 percent per year. This is pretty common, and you may want to push for the lower end of the scale on this.
- *Are the nets included?* What are the actual operating costs of the nets?

I would try to push for a modified gross type lease where you are responsible for the rent and, if necessary, the utilities. This protects you from rising taxes and other operational expenses of the building.

One tactic that I have used successfully is to ask for free rent. Explaining that my business is somewhat seasonal, I agreed to pay the asked for price per square foot, but asked for free rent in July and August on both years of the lease. The landlord's counter offer was free rent one month of the year in exchange for a 3 percent raise of the rent in the second year. It's all give and take, but at the end of the negotiation, I still came out saving thousands of dollars on the lease.

By doing my homework, the big picture came into focus for me. The building had been empty for at least a year and was owned by a person, not a corporation, which meant he didn't have the deep pockets to keep the place empty forever.

If you hear someone say this is a "standard lease," understand that this is salesman double talk. Everything can be negotiated. Do some extra reading, and it will pay off.

WHAT TO LOOK FOR IN A COMMERCIAL SPACE

- *Location:* This is huge. Is it in a good location for teaching? Don't be shortsighted and grab the lowest price. Remember, a nice location with good foot traffic or signage can pay for itself quite easily.

- *Parking:* Is there good available parking? Remember people *hate* walking more than fifty feet for anything. My first commercial location was great for accommodating a modest number of students. After growing the business however, the lack of parking became an issue. (We were in a downtown area with no drive up.)

- *Complementary businesses:* Are there any businesses in the area that complement yours, such as businesses that offer kids activities, music stores (that don't give lessons), martial arts, or dance studios?

- *Noise:* Who are your neighbors on each wall? Downstairs? Upstairs? Despite the smiles, most realtors or landlords aren't crazy about renting to music lessons studios. You must assure them that noise will not be an issue. It's important not to be surrounded by businesses that disturb your lessons.

- *Vibe:* Does this place feel right? Without getting too esoteric, some places just don't have the mojo. Despite this, don't let something easily changed, like paint color or a lighting fixture (easy and inexpensive fixes), deter you.

- *Condition of space:* Is the paint fresh? Do the carpets need replacing?

- *Airflow:* How does the heat and AC work? Try it out. A teacher who owned a commercial recording studio told me, "You can have the greatest gear and engineers, but if the place can't stay hot or cool, it doesn't matter."

- *Windows:* Are the windows (if you have any) sealed? Can you get fresh air?

- *How do the other businesses look?* Healthy? In disrepair? You can learn a lot from poking around.

Take pictures or video of the space. If you are looking at several in a day, you will quickly forget the details. Take notes, and do not hesitate to check again before leasing.

Remember to calculate how much money it will take to get you in this space. Moving can be expensive, and there are always forgotten, or unknown expenses to cover.

CHAPTER 8 TAKEAWAYS

- If you decide to lease commercial space, measure twice and cut once.

- Do your homework before signing a lease!

It's important to stay focused in this business. I've seen people who are good teachers get complacent and stop giving the same type of effort they showed when they started. Spend time evaluating what you do and how you do it. Why do you lose students? Why do students stay for long periods of time? Often, the reason they give for quitting lessons isn't exactly true. Try to figure out what the real reason is.

It is critical to bring your "A" game to work every day. This enthusiasm will build tremendous goodwill with students and parents. It is critical to remember that teaching lessons is not merely an exchange of your time for money. Developing a relationship with your students and having a real interest in who they are and what they do will make your lessons easier. Constantly challenge students and find ways to make what you are doing interesting to them. You may not be a perfect fit for a particular student, but don't take this hard. If you do everything you can to keep your students engaged, then you know that they were not lost to complacency.

THE BEST THINGS IN LIFE ARE FREE ...MOSTLY

Most of the advice in this book does not cost a lot of money to implement. It just takes the commitment to do it. A well-run studio doesn't require great sums of money and an unlimited budget; it can be accomplished mostly with sweat equity and commitment of time. Having an unlimited budget or tons of money usually makes things worse. A "scarcity" mentality in business stimulates your imagination and forces you to resolve issues, rather than just throwing money around indiscriminately.

Be patient! Some of the concepts I have outlined in this book may not work for your situation. Sometimes, learning what doesn't work opens up the door for ideas that do. I have known many people who run their studios in different ways based on location, situation, etc., and have achieved great results. Amplify what works and eliminate what doesn't. Keep track of what you are doing and ask, why did it work?

CONCLUSION

I hope you have found the information in this book useful. There are many ways to play this game, and there are many people who have run different models who have been very successful. I am constantly looking for new ways to make our business stronger and to better serve our clients. There's an expression "All eyes, all ears, all the time." This is good advice. You may find one little thing that works and makes a big difference, either in the internal part of your business, or the external part of your business.

Use this book! Don't just read it and forget to follow up. Applying these principles takes time and commitment.

Check out MikeMcAdam.com for more information, including my blog on music teaching, and some bonus material. If you read this book and need more information or are stuck, I do offer consulting for fellow music teachers.

Suggested Reading

Always try to sharpen your business skills as well as your musical skills. The world is constantly changing and the more you can stay ahead, the more you can anticipate what is coming next. Here are some books that I have found helpful and in many ways illustrate in detail some of the areas we have discussed in this book.

RECOMMENDED TEACHING BOOKS

Here are the top ten books that I use in my studio.

Denyer, Ralph. *The Guitar Handbook*. New York: Knopf, 1992. This book is a great reference book and has lots of additional information on gear and famous players.

des Pres, Josquin. *Guitar Fitness: An Exercising Handbook*. Milwaukee: Hal Leonard Corp., 1992. This book has just about every warm-up exercise you could imagine. These can keep a student busy for a while.

Easy Pop Melodies. (Series) Milwaukee: Hal Leonard Corp. There are several volumes of these books and they are great for simple melodic reading.

Fewell, Garrison. *Jazz Improvisation for Guitar: A Melodic Approach*. Boston: Berklee Press, 1986. Great book for jazz soloing. Uses more of a triad approach that breaks out of the normal "scale for everything" method.

Finn, Jon. *Advanced Modern Rock Guitar Improvisation*. Pacific, MO: Mel Bay, 1999. Jon has a very clear yet humorous way of explaining modes and their application. Just when you think you have this figured out, he puts new twists on them.

Leavitt, William. *Classical Studies for Pick-Style Guitar*. Boston: Berklee Press, 2005. The next step after the Oakes book. Great for sight-reading and etude study.

McAdam, Mike. *Absolute Beginner Guitar*. The last word on guitar teaching. The greatest book on guitar teaching, ever. Of course, I'll pitch my own book! Seriously, my book has a good combination of warm-ups, first position reading, rhythms, common chord progressions, and strumming patterns that I have used with hundreds of students of all ages for over a decade.

Oakes, David. *Music Reading for Guitar: The Complete Method*. Hollywood: Musicians Institute Press, 1998. This book teaches reading in the fifth position. This is really effective for intermediate students who play better than they read.

The Real Book (Series). Milwaukee: Hal Leonard Corp. If you don't already own these, pick them up. There are several volumes filled with information to teach and analyze.

Schroeder, Carl and Keith Wyatt. *Harmony and Theory: A Comprehensive Source for All Musicians*. Hollywood: Musicians Institute Press, 1988. This book does a great job covering theory basics and works its way up to key centers, modes, subdominant chords, etc.

ON RUNNING A PRIVATE LESSONS STUDIO

Johnston, Philip. *PracticeSpot Guide to Promoting Your Teaching Studio*. Pearce, Australia: PracticeSpot, 2003. This book has many great "sweat equity" ideas to get your studio going. Phillip has a high-energy style that is contagious.

Newsam, David R., and Barbara Sprague Newsam. *Making Money Teaching Music*. Cincinnati, OH: Writer's Digest, 1995. Dave does a great job covering the many aspects of the teaching business. Really makes you get the most out of what you have.

TAXES

Fishman, Stephen. *Deduct It! Lower Your Small Business Taxes.* Berkeley: Nolo, 2011.

Wheelwright, Tom. *Tax-Free Wealth: How to Build Massive Wealth by Permanently Lowering Your Taxes.* Minden, NV: BZK, 2012. Once you are doing well with your business, taxes are the single biggest expense and most critical area to get educated in.

GENERAL BUSINESS

Chandler, Steve, and Sam Beckford. *9 Lies That Are Holding Your Business Back: ... and the Truth That Will Set It Free.* Franklin Lakes, NJ: Career, 2005. Great advice that flies in the face of the conventional idea that the business that has the cheapest price wins.

Ferriss, Timothy. *The 4-Hour Work Week: Escape 9-5, Live Anywhere and Join the New Rich.* Chatham: Vermilion, 2011. Mind-blowing book that may change the way you think about everything. This book is very in depth and may seem at first pass to be only minimally applicable to your business. The advice for time management, among other things, is gold.

Fishman, Stephen. *Working for Yourself: Law & Taxes for Independent Contractors, Freelancers & Consultants.* Berkeley, CA: Nolo, 2011. This book may be the first you want to read. Great information on taxing, healthcare for self-employed, business structuring, etc. This was invaluable for me when I started and is regularly updated.

Fried, Jason, and David Heinemeier Hansson. *Rework.* New York: Crown Business, 2010. Sometimes bigger isn't better, better is better. This book made me really look inside my business and work on the little things.

Godin, Seth. *Purple Cow: Transform Your Business by Being Remarkable.* New York: Portfolio, 2003. In a world of boring businesses (white cows), what makes yours stand out (purple cows)? Easy-to-apply ideas that are applicable to any business.

Kaufman, Josh. *The Personal MBA: Master the Art of Business.* New York, NY: Portfolio/Penguin, 2012. Josh's book is a great overall view of business and brings many different sources together. Well done and a great read.

COMMERCIAL REAL ESTATE

De Roos, Dolf. *Real Estate Riches: How to Become Rich Using Your Banker's Money.* New York: Warner, 2001. What if you want to just buy your own commercial property?

Portman, Janet, Fred Steingold, and Janet Portman. *Negotiate the Best Lease for Your Business.* Berkeley, CA: Nolo, 2005. Worth the read to learn the finer points of how to get the best deal on your commercial property.

ADVERTISING

Geddes, Brad. *Advanced Google Ad Words.* Hoboken, NJ: Wiley, 2010. A constantly changing game that we all have to learn to play.

Levinson, Jay Conrad, Jeannie Levinson, and Amy Levinson. *Guerrilla Marketing: Easy and Inexpensive Strategies for Making Big Profits from Your Small Business.* Boston, MA: Houghton Mifflin, 2007.

WEALTH BUILDING

DeMarco, M. J. *The Millionaire Fastlane: Crack the Code to Wealth and Live Rich for a Lifetime!* Phoenix, AZ: Viperion Corporation, 2011. Wild book that challenges the "get rich slow" mantra of the media. Despite sensationalistic title, DeMarco gives some really good advice for a society obsessed with consumerism and consumption. Great ideas about value offerings and how to create them.

Kiyosaki, Robert T., and Sharon L. Lechter. *Rich Dad, Poor Dad: What the Rich Teach Their Kids about Money—That the Poor and Middle Class Do Not!* New York: Warner Business, 2000. The original Rich Dad book. This one sets the foundation for the rest of the series and may ask you to look hard at how you view money.

Kiyosaki, Robert T., and Sharon L. Lechter. *Rich Dad's Cashflow Quadrant: Rich Dad's Guide to Financial Freedom.* New York: Warner Business, 2000. I actually like this book better than the first because it really expanded on the ideas of the first book and offered a definite structure that is easy to follow and use.

Stanley, Thomas J., and William D. Danko. *The Millionaire Next Door: The Surprising Secrets of America's Wealthy.* Atlanta, GA: Longstreet, 1996. Classic report on who the wealthy really are and how they spend and save. A real eye-opener.

INDEX

Page numbers in *italics* indicate illustrations or figures.

ABOUT THE AUTHOR

Photo by Sid Ceaser (ceaserphotography.com)

Mike McAdam has been teaching guitar since 1994. He is a graduate of Berklee College of Music and has played on dozens of records and released three solo titles. He has been the school director at North Main Music in Nashua and Bedford, New Hampshire since its founding in 2003. Mike also runs the guitar department at Rivier University in Nashua, NH. He is the author of *Absolute Beginner Guitar.*

More Fine Publications from BERKLEE PRESS

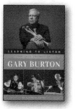